RESEARCHING THE CITY

In memory of Terry Callier (1945–2012)

Los Angeles | London | New Delhi
Singapore | Washington DC

RESEARCHING THE CITY

edited by KEVIN WARD

Los Angeles | London | New Delhi
Singapore | Washington DC

SAGE Publications Ltd
1 Oliver's Yard
55 City Road
London EC1Y 1SP

SAGE Publications Inc.
2455 Teller Road
Thousand Oaks, California 91320

SAGE Publications India Pvt Ltd
B 1/I 1 Mohan Cooperative Industrial Area
Mathura Road
New Delhi 110 044

SAGE Publications Asia-Pacific Pte Ltd
3 Church Street
#10-04 Samsung Hub
Singapore 049483

Editor: Robert Rojek
Editorial assistant: Keri Dickens
Production editor: Katherine Haw
Copyeditor: Elaine Leek
Indexer: Elizabeth Ball
Marketing manager: Michael Ainsley
Cover design: Francis Kenney
Typeset by: C&M Digitals (P) Ltd, Chennai, India
Printed by: CPI Group (UK) Ltd, Croydon, CR0 4YY

Library of Congress Control Number: 2013936829

British Library Cataloguing in Publication data

A catalogue record for this book is available from
the British Library

MIX
Paper from
responsible sources
FSC
www.fsc.org   FSC® C013604

ISBN 978-1-4462-0210-4
ISBN 978-1-4462-0211-1 (pbk)

CONTENTS

LIST OF FIGURES AND TABLES

Figures

Table

CONTRIBUTORS

Allan Cochrane is Professor of Urban Studies in the Faculty of Social Sciences at the Open University. His research interests lie at the intersection of geography and public policy, and he has researched and published on a wide range of topics relating to urban and regional policy.

Bradley L. Garrett is a Researcher in Technological Natures at the University of Oxford with an interest in uncovering hidden places in soil, seas, cities and space. Brad's research interests revolve around issues concerning urban life, place, ruins and waste, spatial politics, subversive social practices, heritage and using multimedia methodologies to critically (and beautifully) interrogate these issues.

Annette Hastings is Senior Lecturer and Leader of the Neighbourhoods and Well-being Research Group in Urban Studies, School of Social and Political Sciences, University of Glasgow. Her research is focused on understanding the causes, consequences and responses to urban inequality. She is particularly interested in how public service provision can sustain inequalities, in whether and how regeneration interventions can address the fundamental problems of disadvantaged neighbourhoods, and in how language use operates to sustain power in the policy process.

Alan Latham is Senior Lecturer in Geography in the Department of Geography, University College London. His research interests are in urban sociality and public life.

Kate Swanson is Associate Professor of Geography, San Diego State University, California, United States. Her research currently focuses on poverty, migration and marginality in Latin America and the US/Mexico border region.

Nik Theodore is a Professor in the Department of Urban Planning and Policy, University of Illinois at Chicago. His research focuses on economic restructuring and urban informality.

Kevin Ward is Professor of Human Geography in the School of Environment and Development at the University of Manchester. His research interests lie in the geographies and histories of urban policy mobilities, state re-organization, and the politics of urban and regional development.

Stephen V. Ward is Professor of Planning History at Oxford Brookes University. He has written widely on historical topics in the field of planning, making extensive use of archival sources. His current research focuses on the historical dimension of the international circulation of ideas and practice in planning and related policy fields.

Matthew Wilson is Assistant Professor of Geography in the Department of Geography at the University of Kentucky, and both Visiting Assistant Professor, Graduate School of Design, and Visiting Scholar, Center for Geographic Analysis, Harvard University, USA. His current research interests are in the social and political implications of geographic information technologies, and specifically in the proliferation of locative media for consumer handheld devices.

ACKNOWLEDGEMENTS

The thinking behind this edited volume arose out of many years of supervising undergraduate and graduate level dissertations on 'urban' issues, broadly defined, in Geography at the University of Manchester in the UK. Conversations with colleagues around the world also suggested that my experiences were not unique. During this period a vast number of companions, edited collections, guides and readers were published on the discipline of geography's approaches, its histories, its methods and its practices. While some were better than others, all proved at least partially useful for my students. At the same time a number of books were published more squarely on the dissertation as a research project. These were often more general, social science books. Again, these proved useful to the geography students I advised, as they struggled over twelve months to produce a substantial piece of independent research. There was little guidance on how to research the city, however.

In addition to this emergence of a body of work that focused explicitly on approaches and methods to producing geographical research, there were also a growing number of student-oriented publications on the city or the urban. From sole authored monographs whose target audience was other academics, through to jointly written, more introductory textbooks, it seemed to me – and to my students – that there was no shortage of literature (in geography and in cognate disciplines such as planning and sociology) on the history of studies of the urban. While substantively useful for the students who saw me to talk about their work, these rarely ever seemed to discuss the methods that were used to generate the research they reported. This seemed to be another omission.

At the interface of these fields – one on approaches and methods in general and one on urban studies – lay the proposal that went off to Sage at the end of 2010, and on the basis of which they commissioned the writing of this book. In the production of this edited collection I have accrued some intellectual debts, and it is time to acknowledge these. Thank you to the referees who passed comment on the proposal. I don't know who you are but the book is better for your insights. Together with the contributors, I have done my best to attend to your concerns. At Sage, Robert Rojek, Sarah-Jayne Boyd, Alana Clogan, Keri Dickens and Katherine Haw have been very encouraging and supportive. I just hope the book sells as you hope! Thanks to Jim Petch and Will Fletcher, who taught the dissertation support classes with me at Manchester, and from whom I learnt an awful lot, particularly about the different ways in which human and physical geographers approach their research.

Closer to home, my debts lie largely with my family members. Colette and Jack have been as supportive as ever and for that I thank them both.

1

INTRODUCTION

Kevin Ward

Beginnings

It began in March 1990 and it ended in February 1991. From start to finish, eleven months of my life was spent on my undergraduate dissertation. Towards the end it felt like I had been working on it for years, not months. I could think of nothing else, as the submission date neared. It had begun, as so many do I think, by me speaking to staff, reading in a rather *ad hoc* and unsystematic manner academic papers on the sorts of issues in which I thought I was interested, and generally thinking about what sort of dissertation I wanted to produce. There was so much choice! How was I ever going to find my way through the literatures? How would I come up with a question or a topic? What methods would I use? How would I know if I had 'enough' data? How would I analyse the 'data'? What counts as 'data'? There were so many questions, these and many others as well, that many times it felt a little overwhelming.

Twenty-two years later it is tempting to believe I knew from the start what I was doing. That I had a plan and that I simply followed it through. The academic that I have become would like to believe that. That would be disingenuous, however. I did not have much of a clue if I am honest. Like many of the undergraduate and graduate students I have advised over the past decade and a half at Manchester, I really had very little idea either of what I wanted to do my dissertation on or how I was going to do it. This was my point of departure in early 1990.

Over the course of the next year I struggled along, grappling with the various geographical theories that academics seemed to be writing to one another about. It appeared I was being drawn to producing a piece of work that lay at the intersection of economic and urban geography, although I am not sure I would have described it like that all those years ago! Debates about economic restructuring, about the successor of Fordism, about something called regulation theory, were all being played out in the journals that I was struggling to find time to read while at the same time meeting the deadlines for coursework submission. I met my adviser on a regular basis, although the support I received was far short of what we offer our students at Manchester. There were no weekly tutorials, no feedback on chapters prior to submission, but rather informal discussions and updates. The summer of 1990 was when I was supposed to do my fieldwork but England's progress to the semi-finals of the World Cup did not help my cause! A number of weeks were lost, and I was playing catch up. The last few months of the year, and of writing up, were predictably stressful. At the time 15,000 words felt like a lot. Structuring the argument, outlining a theoretical perspective, justifying a methodological approach, marshalling the data, pulling through the key arguments and themes – these were all things that I knew constituted a good piece of work but were also all things on which I struggled. The dissertation I submitted received a mark in the mid-60s. At the time I thought it was worth more, but having just re-read it I would say the examiners were generous!

The year 2013

Fast forward just over twenty years and I have subsequently researched and written two master's dissertations and one doctorial dissertation. Many of the issues I faced in each were similar to those I faced in my undergraduate dissertation; from prosaic questions of theory and methods to more mundane concerns over identifying interviewees, organizing fieldwork and checking references. Each dissertation has been longer than the last but has also been easier to research and to write. Over the years I have refined the art of writing a piece of independent research, which probably explains why I do what I do for a living! However, I have not forgotten how hard I found producing my undergraduate and graduate dissertations. I try to bear this in mind when I speak to students at Manchester who are experiencing the same concerns that I had all those years ago. For what I, and Geography at Manchester, expect from a dissertation, whether it be an undergraduate or a graduate piece of work, is not that different from what was expected of me. While there have been many changes in the UK higher education sector over the past three decades in the undergraduate and graduate curriculums – and in other education systems around the world – the dissertation, as a piece of independent and scholarly research, remains largely intact. By and large the substance, the structure and the style of a dissertation is today what it was when I was an undergraduate in the late 1980s/early 1990s and a graduate in the early to late 1990s. In many universities it still makes up a significant element of the overall mark; students still work on it for a year or so, as part of a three- or four-year undergraduate degree programme, or for a number of months for a one- or two-year masters; and it is still something that prospective employers show an interest in at interviews. While it might not be exactly the same all round the world, at least at the undergraduate level, many students are still required to produce a not dissimilar document, in terms of both length and structure.

However, one aspect of producing a dissertation that has changed quite dramatically over the past twenty years or so is that, back then, there was very little academic literature to turn to for help. Most of the approaches or methods pieces I drew upon in my undergraduate and graduate dissertations were those written by academics *for* academics, and there were not many of them. Now there is a mass of books written specifically for those students who are required to produce dissertations for their degrees. Think of the books you know about, the ones you are assigned on methods and philosophies classes, or which are recommended to you to help you research and write your dissertation. Some are in geography, others in cognate disciplines, such as anthropology or sociology. Many, indeed, describe themselves as 'social sciences' textbooks, transcending individual disciplines such as geography. It is possible to organize them into four groups, although there are plenty of overlaps, as one might expect.

The first group are those books that outline the various histories and geographies of the discipline in the context of the claim made by Heffernan (2003: 3) that '[t]here is no single history of "geography", only a bewildering variety of different, often competing versions of the past'. These explore the emergence of the discipline and its evolution over the years. They examine the ways in which new thinking emerged in the discipline, such as that around the quantitative revolution in the 1960s or cultural studies in the 1990s, and what this meant for the discipline, from the methods that geographers began to use to what counted as 'data' (Johnston and Sidaway 2004). Some highlight the internal differences within the discipline, most noticeably between human and physical geography. They provide some historical context to the production of your dissertation, hopefully making you aware of how the research that now gets done under the name of 'geography' has changed over the years.

The second set of books that will be useful to you in the process of producing a dissertation are those that focus on the approaching and researching of geography (Aitken and Valentine 2006; Castree et al. 2005; Cloke et al. 2004; Flowerdew and Martin 2005a; Hoggart et al. 2002; Kitchin and Tate 2000). In these the emphasis tends to be on the philosophies and theories that characterize the current discipline. From these collections and compendiums you get a real sense of the diversity of geography. For all students this is both an opportunity and a challenge. The relative breadth of the contemporary discipline means that students have plenty of potential dissertation topics from which to choose. It also means that where geography starts and stops is not always clear. The same can be said about what constitutes the 'right' theories and the 'right' methods. For many students the uncertainty they sometimes feel in their courses is exacerbated in the production of their dissertations. Perhaps it is something you feel? As Flowerdew and Martin (2005a: 1) put it, '[y]ou may currently see your project as a large, and somewhat frightening, chore or you may welcome it as an opportunity to express originality and get out of the classroom.'

A third set of publications are those on the key concepts and thinkers in the discipline (Clifford et al. 2009; Hubbard et al. 2004). These tend to consist of a larger number of shorter individual contributions. They are useful reference points for those of you who are looking for a place to start; they will help you to find out more about the core of the discipline and the key individuals whose work over the years has shaped the evolution of geography. However, these volumes come with a health warning. In reflecting on their own choices in *Key Concepts in Geography*, Holloway et al. (2003: xv) note they are 'inevitably partial, reflecting the contested nature of the discipline in which we all work and study'. Like the pulling together of all edited collections, the content says something about the editors as well as about the content itself.

The fourth and final set of works that have been produced over the past couple of decades are those on the managing of a research project, such as a dissertation (Greetham 2009; Rudestam and Newton 2001; Smith et al. 2009; Walliman 2004). With some exceptions, such as Flowerdew and Martin (2005a), many of these reach out beyond the discipline. Most are geared towards a social science student audience. As such, they consist of general guidance to students like yourselves who are undertaking a significant piece of independent research. They cover issues such as preparing for your dissertation, collecting and analysing data, time management, and the production of the final piece of work. So, the emphasis is on both the academic and the personal skills required to successfully produce an undergraduate and graduate dissertation, inside and outside of geography.

Taken together these contributions offer you a resource that simply did not exist prior to the very late 1990s/early 2000s. At that time something stirred amongst publishers and academics and the result has been a steep upswing in the number of books in this field. It is within this body of work, much of which deals with the 'how to ...' questions that students often ask those of us who advise on dissertations, that this book sits. For while the various generalist edited collections of the sort just discussed have much to offer students, the focus of this book is squarely on the researching of cities. Every year in Geography at Manchester between forty and fifty undergraduate students study for what, broadly, might be understood as 'urban' dissertations. These explore issues such as climate change, consumption, cosmopolitanism, crime, economic development, media, regeneration, retail and transport. Conversations with other colleagues around the world suggest that Manchester is not atypical. We also have a number of graduate students whose dissertations are similarly focused on urban issues. While there are significant differences between undergraduate and graduate dissertations, there are also some similarities. The standard expected from the latter is higher than the former, obviously. However, both tend to consist of a mix of theory, methods and empirics and both require analytical and management skills.

Over the years what has become clear, through conversations with students, is that they find researching the city a challenge, intellectually and organizationally. Specifically, they wrestle with how to understand a city in all of its complexity, and its relationship to terms such as urbanization. While these can sometimes be seen as rather abstract concerns by many students, they are nevertheless important issues because understanding what they mean matters to planning and delivering an undergraduate and graduate dissertation.

Researching *the city*

So what constitutes 'the city'? What is the relationship between the city, the urban and urbanization? How should you make sense of the complexity of the city? What role do you want 'the city' to play in your dissertation? These – alongside a host of others – are the sorts of questions that many undergraduate and graduate students around the world ask, of themselves, their peers, and of staff, as they grapple with their dissertations. You are probably not so different! It is worth just reflecting on what you mean when you talk about 'the city' and how this fits with the vast amount of work produced by academics of one theoretical persuasion or another from across a host of disciplines, including but not restricted to, geography.

Historically the city has been differentiated from the village or the town according to size and population density (Hubbard 2006; Saunders 1986). Something was labelled 'the city' and everything else was 'the other'. The larger the grouping of people together on a single site the more it was understood to exhibit city-like characteristics. In some countries, settlements were anointed as cities according to some proxy of economic or political power; the city was a territory, within which the co-presence of people in close proximity to one another led to the establishment of certain cultures and mores. So, a series of experiences, of living and working, became labelled as urban cultures. Some were progressive, others less so. In his classic study of industrial Manchester – the city from where I am writing this chapter – Engels (1845) writes about the emergence of the first industrial city. He argued that it led to terrible living conditions for workers but also offered these same workers through their close proximity to one another the possibility of joining together to challenge the still-emerging capitalist system. This is about more than just physical layout, more than just the infrastructure of roads, sewers and wires that allow the city to exist; it is about the very rhythm and tempo to the city, about the comings and goings of cars, of finance, of people, which sustain it as a place to live and visit, to work and to play. While cities were discrete, largely bounded territories, 'urbanization' refers to the system-wide relationships between cities. About more than just individual settlements, urbanization referred to the qualitative conditions that characterize relationships within and between cities; it was concerned with the sort of labour markets that Theodore (Chapter 6, this volume) writes about, or the built environments that Garrett (Chapter 10, this volume) explores in his chapter. And at the beginning of the twenty-first century, with more than half of the world's population living in cities, talk has now turned to an 'urban age' (Smith 2012). Acknowledging that the fastest growing cities continue to be located in South and East Asia and Africa, this term sought to capture the growing number of large cities around the world. In this vein, and drawing on the work of sociologist Henri Lefebvre (1970), notions of planetary urbanization have been used to capture not just the number of cities and their size at the current moment, but the on-going cultural, economic and social transformations that are rendering more and more sites around the globe 'urban'. This is about the speed, scale and scope of urbanization that has fundamentally changed the character of urban areas. Thinking about cities as territories clearly has implications for how you study them. It suggests that you do not take for granted the city as a territory.

More recent work on cities within the social sciences, including geography, has questioned the territorial assumptions that underpin much of this earlier work. According to Amin (2004: 34) 'cities come with no automatic promise of territorial ... integrity, since they are made through the spatiality of flow, juxtaposition, porosity and relational connectivity.' Drawing on work by Massey (1993, 2004), this perspective argues that 'cities exist in an era of increasing geographically extended spatial flows' (Jacobs 2012: 412). That is, cities as entities to study don't respect the formal boundaries assigned to them through governments. The relations, between institutions or people, stretch out across space. Often these relations bring places that are geographically distant closer together. As a result, this relational way of thinking about cities argues that the contemporary city needs to be conceptualized as 'open, discontinuous, relational and internally diverse' (Allen et al. 1998: 143). This also has implications for how you go about researching cities. It suggests you don't take for granted the city as a territory. Where do you study the city in which you are interested? Inside or outside of the city, or perhaps, do you try to trace out some of the networks of which the city is part? Or, if you are interested in migration, do you look at where people have come from as well as from where they have travelled?

Of course, for those of you considering how to understand a particular city as part of the initial stage in planning your dissertation, there is some theoretical middle ground. It is possible to understand cities both as territories and as sites of relations with elsewhere. For MacLeod and Jones (2007: 1186) 'all contemporary expressions of territory ... are, to varying degrees, punctuated by and orchestrated through a myriad of trans-territorial networks and relational webs of connectivity.' So contemporary cities do have boundaries of sorts – although they are open to contestation and manipulation. Many times these stem from government entities, in areas of policy such as education, health or policing. These boundaries also appear on maps of one sort or another. They are not natural, however. Rather, and much like any boundaries, they are the outcome of various decisions over many years. And they are not fixed. Moreover, these boundaries are in part constituted through relations that cities have with other cities: cities are nodes in wider flows of ideas, finances, people and so on. So the city you may been interested in studying for your dissertation may be involved in a number of different sorts of networks and relations with other cities, some shorter, others longer, some more important for your study, others less so. As a minimum, as you think about your dissertation you need to be clear about how you are going to understand cities in general, and what that means for how you are going to study your city or cities in particular. Of course, this also necessitates that you think about the methods you want to use in your dissertation.

Researching the city

If appreciating the different ways in which the 'city' is understood is important for those of you setting out to do an urban dissertation, so too is thinking about how to research the city. Many of you will have had some classes on methods as part of the dissertation support provided by your department or school. The most popular methods amongst recent cohorts at Manchester are questionnaires and semi-structured interviews. Ethnography and participation observation are also used by some students. Each method requires you know some of its advantages and its disadvantages. All have their limits and it is not really possible to say absolutely that one is better than any other. The usefulness or otherwise of a method for your dissertation depends on other decisions you will make, such as where you want to do your research and on what. As will become clearer (I hope) as you read through this book, the method you choose to use in your dissertation should allow you to generate the knowledge you require to answer the questions you have set yourself based on your reading of work produced by academics – that is, your academic literature review.

So, given the complexity of contemporary cities, and their place in different sorts of networks, you need to give serious attention to how you research the city. That may well mean using a range of different methods. There is no absolute 'right' or 'wrong' method to use in a dissertation. This lack of right or wrong can confuse some students, who want to be told what to do. That is wrongheaded. Instead, you should be thinking about your research questions, and what you need to know in order to answer them. That then demands you think about which methods – and there are many, some of which are discussed in the rest of this book – you think will provide you with the sorts of 'data' that you need to answer the questions. Data can come in the form of images, numbers, recordings, and words. Some will be more suited to addressing your questions than others. And, of course, you don't have complete control over the data you generate, regardless of the method or methods you choose. As we will see in Chapter 2, you need to design your research, and an important element of this is acknowledging that the only certainty in doing a dissertation is that there are no certainties! Something unforeseen will happen while you are generating your data. What you can do, though, is to think long and hard about how you research the city, and to think about the link between the kinds of knowledge you need to generate to answer your research questions and the method or methods that are most likely to generate that knowledge.

The rest of the book

Chapter 2 sets the scene for the chapters that follow. It sets out in general terms how to go about undertaking an urban research project, such as an undergraduate or graduate dissertation. It takes the reader through the various stages of the research process. Students often find the notion of 'research' hard to fathom – as rather daunting, as something done by academics, not something they are capable of doing by and for themselves. The purpose of this chapter is to demystify the process of doing research, so that you have a better understanding of the intellectual and personal journey on which you embark when you begin your dissertation. This necessarily means discussing some of the issues that in my experience many students find the least enjoyable aspect of their degrees – philosophies and theories, or 'the isms'. Sorry folks, but there is no way of avoiding these if you are going to be aware of the issues that need to be thought about at the beginning of the dissertation research process, and to which you will return repeatedly over the course of its production.

Chapters 3–10 are each focused on a different way of studying the city. Stephen Ward writes on archives (Chapter 3). He makes it clear that archives are not simply there, waiting to be discovered, but rather the researcher – you – plays an important role in the construction of 'an archive' and the nearly always selective way in which they are drawn upon to generate 'evidence'. Allan Cochrane on interviewing (Chapter 4) outlines two important and different ways in which the city can be understood, and discusses the art of interviewing. As the sociologist Pierre Bourdieu (1996:17) argued a number of years ago, 'If the research interview is different from most of the exchanges of ordinary existence due to its objective of pure knowledge, it is, in all cases, a social relation.' It is a conversation in which the researcher plays an active role in the generation of material, as Allan makes clear. Kate Swanson on ethnography (Chapter 5) uses her own research into street working children in Ecuador. She outlines some of the issues involved in doing ethnographic research, before, during and after being in something called 'the field'. It is clear that this method is both intellectually and personally rewarding. It is also time-consuming! Nik Theodore has many years of experience of researching those that society regards as lying on its margins. He draws on his work on those occupying the lower rungs of the labour market to discuss the uses of questionnaires (Chapter 6) in researching one element of the city and its labour markets. Nik outlines the advantages of this method, particularly when you require numerical 'data' to answer your research questions. Annette Hastings on discourse analysis (Chapter 7) discusses the different ways in which 'words' and the meanings attached to them can be useful for studying the city. In her own research she has explored how certain words and phrases are put to political work in the field of urban regeneration. Chapter 8, by Alan Latham, is on the use of diaries as a research method. Unlike many of the others in this book, this particular method has a shorter history in the social sciences. In his chapter Alan discusses the ways in which diaries have been increasingly used in geography to study the rhythms and routines of people's day-to-day lives. He looks at the origins of this method, what it can reveal about the city that perhaps other methods cannot, and what are its limits. Alan also highlights the emergence of various technologies, particularly GPS (global positioning systems), that are becoming ubiquitous in many devices and that appear to offer a cheap and uniquely detailed avenue for gathering information about people's activities in cities.

The penultimate of the methods chapters is by Matthew Wilson on geographic information systems (GIS), another technology like GPS with a relatively short history. Twenty-five years ago an edited book such as this would not have contained a chapter on GIS. As Matthew makes clear in Chapter 9, this method is relatively new, and GIS actually encapsulates a range of modes of inquiry. His chapter takes you through some of the possible uses of the technology in a dissertation such as the one you will undertake. In Chapter 10 Bradley Garrett turns to photography and video as ways of researching the city. He uses his own PhD project to explore under what sorts of conditions these methods might be suitable for your dissertation. The technology is still relatively new in the discipline of geography, although with a much longer history in other social sciences, and Bradley cautions you to think carefully about in what ways these methods might allow you to answer your research questions. In both Matthew's and Bradley's chapters the message is clear: don't be led by the technology but rather decide how it can be of use to you.

Each of the chapters in this collection is written in the author's own unique style, and so there are differences between them, as perhaps you would expect. And much as there will be differences between the dissertations you will all produce. However, there are also some similarities, deliberately so in order to make it easier for the reader to compare across the chapters. Each one begins with an introduction followed by some discussion of the preparation required for doing research. In some cases the preparation is central to the method, in other cases it is less so, but still important. There is then some discussion of how the author did their research. A range of empirical examples are used, reflecting the interest and the expertise of those doing the writing. Finally, there is some discussion about how to make sense of the data and to link it back to the issues that others write about in the particular existing academic literature. There are some frequently asked questions in relation to each method. These are based on the sorts of questions I have been asked at Manchester, but also, I am told, the sorts of questions colleagues at other universities get asked. There are also some follow-up annotated references, so that those of you who want to can go away and find out more about the method and whether it makes sense for you in the context of your particular research project. These chapters are definitely not the last word on the particular method they discuss. Those of you who are doing dissertations should be looking to go away and find out more about your method of choice and the way it has been used.

Conclusion

The writer T.S. Eliot once said that 'If you start with a bang, you won't end with a whimper'. This comment may have been made in reference to the writing of a novel but it applies equally to the writing of a dissertation. Be upfront. Sell the reader the focus of your work, why it is important and why they should be interested in what you have to say. If you do this then the reader – who will probably also be the marker of your dissertation – will be hooked. Of course, this is easy to say but harder to do. Chapter 11 focuses on the process of writing, and more specifically, on writing up your dissertation. It pulls together the contributions of the various chapters and takes you through the different elements of producing your dissertation. As Boyle (1997: 235) notes, 'it is tempting to assume that the write-up is a relatively simple part of the research process.' Of course, from talking to my undergraduate and graduate students, I know this is often the aspect of the dissertation which they think will take less time than they find it does. This is about the various ways in which you can do justice to all the hard work you have put into reading existing academic literature, organizing and doing your field-work, and analysing your data. It is not something to be left to the last minute, as every year some unfortunate students at Manchester discover!

Regardless of which of the methods covered in this book you have used, you will have to write the different elements up into something called a 'dissertation', and this is the focus of the chapter that follows. Dissertations do not plan or write themselves! They need to be *designed*. Thought needs to be given to the different components of the dissertation and how each one will be managed, often not as a sequential piece of work. Rather, the dissertation needs to be thought about as a series of discrete but interrelated tasks, after each of which you reflect back on your aims and focus accordingly. What you don't do is plough on through your dissertation, not allowing yourself any time to think and to reflect. After all, it is ultimately your piece of work; you are the one with the most invested in it, and it is your degree to which this piece of work will make a sizeable contribution. Oh, and good luck!

References

Aitken, S. and Valentine, G. (eds) (2006) *Approaches to Human Geography*. London: Sage.

Allen, J., Massey, D. and Cochrane, A. with Charlesworth, J., Court, G., Henry, N. and Sarre, P. (1998) *Rethinking the Region: Spaces of Neoliberalism*. London: Routledge.

Amin, A. (2004) Regions unbound: towards a new politics of place. *Geografiska Annaler: Series B, Human Geography*, 86: 33–44.

Bourdieu, P. (1996) Understanding. *Theory, Culture and Society*, 13: 17–37.

Boyle, P. (1997) Writing the report, in R. Flowerdew and D.M. Martin (eds), *Methods in Human Geography: A Guide for Students Doing a Research Project*. Harlow: Pearson Education, pp. 253–53.

Castree, N., Rogers, A. and Sherman, D. (eds) (2005) *Questioning Geography*. Oxford: Blackwell.

Clifford, N.J., Holloway, S., Rice, S. and Valentine, G. (eds) (2009) *Key Concepts in Geography* (2nd edn). London: Sage.

Cloke, P., Crang, P. and Goodwin, M. (eds) (2004) *Envisioning Human Geographies*. London: Arnold.

Engels, F. (1969/1845) *The Condition of the Working Class in England*. London: Panther Books.

Flowerdew, R. and Martin, D.M. (eds) (2005a) *Methods in Human Geography: A Guide for Students Doing a Research Project*. Harlow: Pearson Education.

Flowerdew, R. and Martin, D.M. (2005b) Introduction, in R. Flowerdew and D.M. Martin (eds), *Methods in Human Geography: A Guide for Students Doing a Research Project*. Harlow: Pearson Education, pp. 1–5.

Greetham, B. (2009) *How to Write Your Undergraduate Dissertation*. Basingstoke: Palgrave Macmillan.

Heffernan, M. (2003) Histories of geography, in S. Holloway, S. Rice and G. Valentine (eds), *Key Concepts in Geography*. London: Sage, pp. 3–22.

Hoggart, K., Lees, L. and Davies, A. (2002) *Researching Human Geography*. London: Arnold.

Holloway, S., Rice, S. and Valentine, G. (eds) (2003) *Key Concepts in Geography*. London: Sage.

Hubbard, P. (2006) *City*. London: Routledge.

Hubbard, P., Kitchin, R. and Valentine, G. (2004) *Key Thinkers on Place and Space*. London: Sage.

Jacobs, J. (2012) Urban geographies I: still thinking cities relationally. *Progress in Human Geography*, 36: 412–22.

Johnston, R. and Sidaway, J. (2004) *Geography and Geographers: Anglo-American Human Geography since 1945*. London: Arnold.

Kitchin, R. and Tate, N. (2000) *Conducting Research into Human Geography: Theory, Methodology and Practice*. Harlow: Prentice Hall.

Lefebvre, H. (1970/2003) *The Urban Revolution*. Minneapolis, MN: Minnesota University Press.

MacLeod, G. and Jones, M. (2007) Territorial, scalar, connected, networked: in what sense a 'regional world'. *Regional Studies*, 41: 1177–91.

Massey, D. (1993) Power-geometry and a progressive sense of place, in J. Bird, B. Curtis, T. Putnam, G. Robertson and L. Tickner (eds), *Mapping the Futures: Local Cultures, Global Change*. London: Routledge, pp. 59–69.

Massey, D. (2004) Geographies of responsibility. *Geografiska Annaler: Series B, Human Geography*, 86: 5–18.

Rudestam, K.E. and Newton, R.R. (2001) *Surviving Your Dissertation: A Comprehensive Guide to Content and Process* (2nd edn). London: Sage.

Saunders, P. (1986) *Social Theory and the Urban Question*. London: Routledge.

Smith, K., Todd, M. and Waldman, J. (2009) *Doing Your Undergraduate Social Science Dissertation*. London: Routledge.

Smith, P. (2012) *City: A Guidebook for the Urban Age*. London: Bloomsbury Publishing.

Walliman, N. (2004) *Your Undergraduate Dissertation: The Essential Guide for Success*. London: Sage.

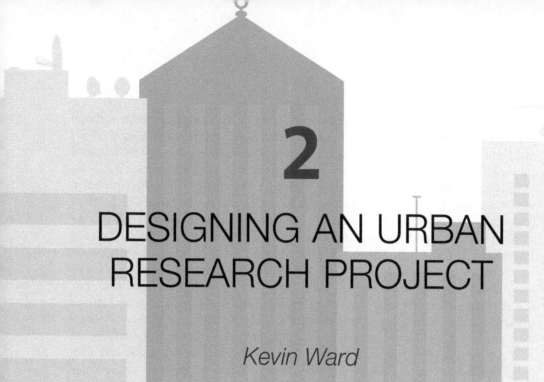

2

DESIGNING AN URBAN RESEARCH PROJECT

Kevin Ward

Don't leave it too late: your life will be a total misery.

The dissertation was where I really got to pursue my own interests and not those of the lecturers.

You realize how hard it is to study things properly.

Introduction

It was with these three unattributed quotes that I would begin the dissertation support classes I used to deliver in Geography at the University of Manchester. They were comments final year students made to me *after* they had completed and submitted their dissertations. Only then, when reflecting back on the whole dissertation process, did they appreciate quite what had been involved, both intellectually and personally. I would also invite one or two final year students into my lectures, to get them to talk to the second year students about the importance of the dissertation and the need to plan in advance. Hearing from students who had literally just finished their dissertation was a welcome addition to having someone like me standing in front of the students. Or, that was what the feedback sheets told me! After all, and as I used to say regularly to my students, a dissertation does not design or manage itself. While this may seem obvious, nevertheless, there is a need for you to acknowledge early on in the research process that producing a dissertation will test not only your intellectual ability; this is something the staff or faculty at your own institution will stress I am sure. Your capacity to manage, organize and plan will also be important if you are to deliver your dissertation on time. An important first step in preparing yourself to produce a dissertation is acknowledging that as a project it consists of different but connected elements. This should make the dissertation seem less daunting. If you are worried – as many students are – about producing a dissertation of anything between 10,000 and 20,000 words then breaking it down into smaller mini-projects should allay some of your fears. Hopefully you will be aware of some, if not all, of the elements from the dissertation support classes provided by your own institution. The main ones are the reviewing of existing academic literature and the generating of research questions; the planning and designing of the research; the gathering, generating and analysing of data; and the writing up of the dissertation. However, do not be fooled by the way they are listed here. You do not do one, tick a box and then move on. Each of these elements is interrelated and they are revisited a number of times while you are producing your dissertation. You will be reviewing the existing academic literature almost up to the day you hand in your dissertation, while writing it is not something that should get left to the last minute (see Chapter 11, this volume). Indeed, as soon as you start making notes to yourself about possible topics, or writing down keywords based on the work of academics, you are officially 'writing' your dissertation!

This chapter provides a very short overview of the process of designing an urban research project. There are a number existing social science textbooks that take the reader through a research project, such as a dissertation. These are worth turning to if you want more details of any of the different stages (Smith et al. 2009; Walliman 2004). This chapter takes you quickly through the different elements up to what you do with the data you have generated. It gives you a flavour of the sorts of issues you should be thinking about as you design your dissertation. These apply to most if not all types of dissertations, and thus this chapter provides a general set of comments before the following eight chapters turn to different ways of studying the city, and the specific issues this raises. The final chapter turns to what you do with your data once you have generated it and how you write through your dissertation, pulling together all the different elements into a coherent document of which you can be proud.

Planning your dissertation

A dissertation is an intellectual project. In the raft of textbooks that have been produced for students like you a great deal of emphasis is placed on the intellectual element, in terms of the dissertation's theoretical content, its contribution to knowledge and its empirical findings. That is not surprising. Most of the contributions are written by those trained in disciplines in which issues of theory, philosophy and methods are standard fare. Likewise, in my experience, the sort of dissertation support you will receive at your own institution will focus largely, but not exclusively, on the intellectual bit. However, it is also important to acknowledge that your dissertation is a project, and as such, requires planning – and the use of 'planning' here refers to the listing and ordering of the various aspects of the dissertation, and the informed assessment of the potential risks of each and how these risks will be either negated or managed. Universities increasingly require anyone conducting research to complete ethics and risk assessment documentation. Yours is unlikely to be any different. The paperwork is time-consuming but important and time should be taken on its completion. However, here we are talking about 'risk' more broadly. It refers to anything that may or may not happen when you – the student – need it to happen as part of the dissertation process. These can be very ordinary and mundane things, such as having to wait to get hold of a book that someone else has taken out of the library. Alternatively, it can be more important, such as not knowing who to interview in order to answer your research questions, or, having identified who you need to speak to, not being able to convince them to give up their time to meet you.

When you list and order the different elements of the dissertation it is important that you think about sequence and size, before moving on to risks. Put simply, not all the things on the list you produce will take the same amount of time! You need to think about the labour involved at each of the four main stages of the dissertation, probably breaking down each element into sub-elements and begin attaching a time to each. That makes the production of timelines easier. So, how will you go about pulling together the various literatures you want/need to read? How will you generate a questionnaire or an interview schedule? How will you analyse your material? How long will each of these take and what are the risks associated with each? These are the sorts of question you need to ask yourself as you begin to plan your dissertation; they are important as they may make some dissertations less or more appropriate, given the expectations of your own institution.

According to Ragin (1994: 191):

> Research design is a plan for collecting and analyzing evidence that will make it possible for the investigator to answer whatever questions he or she has posed. The design of an investigation touches almost all aspects of the research, from the minute details of data collection to the selection of the techniques of data analysis.

Like all 'plans', of course, it can go wrong, horribly wrong! I say this not to scare you, but simply to make the point that your dissertation is about you and your relationship with the world in all manner of ways. And, as we all know, the world does not always behave in the way we would like it to! So at every stage of the dissertation process there are risks. In part what is important from the beginning is that you acknowledge there are risks, outline what they are and then plan to negate them as far as you can. The key here is *anticipation* and *preparedness*. That is, thinking ahead and seeing risks before they manifest themselves and having in place a set of clear responses.

In this light, it is possible to identify three main types of risks. The first is *people-related risks*. As Kennedy notes, '*you* must be interested in the project at the outset' (1999: 128, original emphasis). So, a people risk is that you lack the interest in your dissertation topic, which manifests itself in a lack of application and motivation. This makes the work you do on deciding a topic and honing the research questions particularly important. A dissertation is an independent piece of work. Even at those institutions where the level of support is high, there will still be plenty of times when you will be working by yourself. Another people risk is that you set the bar too high. Being heroic has no place in producing a dissertation; better to be realistic when setting goals and to achieve them. For most students the time allowed to produce a dissertation is not enough to learn a new language, for example, so do not think you can factor this in when deciding on the location of your fieldwork. Ensure that you either have or can acquire relatively easily the skills required to deliver your dissertation. The same goes for the technical skills required to analyse large datasets. Can you write the software program you need? If you don't have the skills at the beginning of the dissertation process when are you going to acquire them?

Process-related risks, such as setting unachievable goals, or assuming that the type of data you require is easily accessible, constitute the second type of risks of which you need to be aware. Students who plan to work with existing data sometimes assume it is easier to get hold of than it is, or assume that it will be in the form in which they need it. Instead, students often have to re-work pre-constructed data, as well as being aware of 'the why, the how and also the when and where' (Cloke et al. 2004: 37) of the data construction. If the dataset was assembled for a different purpose or for a different audience what do you need to do to it for it to be useful for your dissertation? And, if you are relying on someone else providing your data there is a risk that they will not deliver the goods. In this case, do you have a plan B? Another process-related risk is the accessing of materials of different sorts, the origins of which are a long way from where you are studying. While not all universities have the same level of resources, generally the literature you seek will be accessible through various on-line catalogues and search engines. Of course, even if you happen to be a student at one of the best-resourced universities in the world, it is unlikely that you will be able to access all the literatures you want on-site! So, at some stage it is likely you are going to have to order (and wait) for certain resources, or spend time working out how to access certain on-line archives or resources. There is always the risk that the documents don't appear – then what?

The third type of risk is *technology-related risks*. These come in various guises. Whatever your dissertation, there is always the possibility that files can be lost: deleted, corrupted or quite literally lost. So, back up your work – not once, but twice (or even three times: the stakes are that high!) – and don't keep all the copies in one place. I once had a student working with me who had three electronic copies of his work, which you might think was good practice but they were *all* in his car when it was stolen a couple of weeks before he was due to submit his dissertation! You may also be using software to generate and analyse data. These programs take time to learn. You need to make sure you know what you are going to do with your data once you have generated it. This demands a degree of technical expertise – and you need to be confident from the beginning that you will get the support as and when you need it. So, for example, if you know you are going to use questionnaires in your dissertation, do you know what sorts of data will be produced and do you know how you will analyse it? If you don't, will there be someone at your institution who can help you over the summer when you want to run your models? You also need to ensure that you understand the statistics/mathematics behind the sorts of numbers produced by software packages, as the assumptions underpinning the data will need to be explained in your dissertation.

Having outlined the various elements to your dissertation and assigned each one the time you believe is needed to complete it, perhaps in the form of a timescale with a series of milestones, and then thought about the risk attached to each, the next step is slowly starting the process. In turning to reading the work of others and producing a series of research questions, exploring the types of methods it might make sense to use given the focus of your dissertation, and then exploring the kinds of data you will produce and how you will analyse them, you will also return to your milestones. It is fine to modify these. The timescale is not set in stone; rather it is a 'live' document, one that reflects where you are in the dissertation process and your informed expectations about what comes next. However, and that said, the end of the timescale is fixed. That is the date for the dissertation to be submitted!

Starting your dissertation

According to Flick (2011: 32), 'you should begin your research by reading'. This is good advice and something that a number of my students appear to ignore each year! In my experience some students put themselves under enormous pressure when thinking about what should be the focus of their dissertation. Every year I have students come to see me, stuck, unable to decide on what to do for their dissertation. I ask them what they have done so far. A number seem to have sat at a table, in the library or at home, and simply tried to will a dissertation topic/title into being! Many seem to forget the basic skills they have honed in producing pieces of coursework. Instead, sitting on their own, they find it hard to produce – almost out of thin air – a focus for their dissertation. Looking at blank sheets of paper can be disempowering. Evidence suggests that starting the dissertation is something that is found particularly difficult by many UK students (Harrison and Whalley 2008). Moving from not knowing to knowing what you would like to do your dissertation on is too important to be left to chance, however, and so you need to devise some strategies. Break down the process into clear steps that get you from where you are to where you need to be. Write a list of things that could help you along. And it is not only topic selection that can prove troublesome. While thinking about the focus of your dissertation you also need to be thinking about research questions. This involves narrowing down the focus of your dissertation, moving from an often quite general topic to a more specific set of research questions.

Whether seeking to define the focus of your research or to produce some research questions, a useful way of thinking about both is how actually they emerge most easily out of a series of engagements with something or somebody else. It might be an academic article that you have read that interests you, a professor whom you find particularly inspiring, or something that you have heard on the radio or read in a newspaper (Gatrell and Flowerdew 2005). It can be anything from which you can draw some inspiration and insight, and that will allow you to make some informed choices. After all, as Martin and Flowerdew (2005: 35) note, 'There are many possible sources of ideas which can be developed into good research questions [or topics].' In addition to arising out of your relationship with something else, research questions do not come fully formed. They tend to be bitty and disjointed, fragments of questions that you have to put together and take apart, modify and so on over the process of producing your dissertation. Your research questions are not finalized, if that is the right word, until the end. Indeed, the questions will evolve over the course of the dissertation process, which at some institutions can be a whole year. However, and despite acknowledging that they should evolve over time, the first element of producing a dissertation is selecting a focus, broadly understood, and then identifying specific research questions that you intend to address.

If you are reading this book you have already done some work by choosing to research the city. You have chosen a particular focus for your dissertation. However, having decided to undertake an urban project there is still a lot more work to do to decide what it is you want to find out about – that is, the research questions you want to answer. So, there are still some important issues for you to address! Hopefully the rest of this book will help you. However, if you have got to the stage of deciding the focus of your dissertation, it is to be hoped that this has come about in part through the reading advocated by Flick (2011). And, all being well, you will have written notes and reflected on your interactions with something or somebody else. For, as Walliman (2011: 33) explains, the 'narrowing process will require a lot of background reading in order to discover what has been written about the subject already, what research has been carried out, where further work needs to be done and where controversial issues still remain.' As if to reinforce the non-linearity of the research process – that is, the moving back and forth between the different elements – having established a focus for your dissertation, and perhaps established some research questions-in-progress (that is, subject to change), for many of you the next step is to (re)turn to various literatures.

Situating your dissertation

The bottom line is that it is unlikely you will be the first or the last to produce a dissertation in your particular field. However, at times you may feel that what you are doing is truly unique. It probably is in some ways. At other times you may feel like it has all been done before. Again, it probably has in a manner of speaking. These sorts of emotional roller-coasters are not uncommon for students doing a significant piece of work over a number of months or years. Overseeing a research project that means so much to you, literally in terms of its contribution to your overall degree classification, draws on your emotional resources. In my experience students also form a unique bond with their dissertation, sometimes struggling to put some distance between it and them, as they manage other coursework demands. This is something of which to be aware and to manage.

In terms of the 'value added' of your dissertation, one minute you are pushing back the boundaries of knowledge, the next minute you are plodding along producing something that no one would ever possibly want to read. The truth though is somewhere in between. Your work will and will not be unique. To appreciate where your dissertation sits *vis-à-vis* other similar studies you are required to 'situate' your dissertation; this means to place it in its wider context. There are a number of 'wider contexts', the most local, so to speak, being its place alongside other undergraduate or graduate dissertations in your institution. So, it makes sense to have a look through past dissertations to get a feel for the way they look and how they read. Think carefully about when during the process you do this. You want to be informed by the dissertations you read, but you don't want to be led too much by them. So, be clear on what it is you want out of reading the work of previous students before you begin.

Further afield, according to Flick (2011: 35), four 'wider contexts' can be identified. These are:

Theoretical literature about the topic of your study

Methodological literature about how to do your research and how to use the methods you choose

Empirical literature about previous research in the field of your study or similar fields

Theoretical and empirical literature to help contextualize, compare and generalize your findings.

What should strike you immediately is that you need to situate your work in a number of contexts, and that it is not enough just to cite the work of others in your academic context/literature review chapter. The work of others, whether in academic journals, on Internet sites or in newspaper articles, should be cited throughout the text. You are constantly in the throes of comparing your work to others, whether theoretically, methodologically or empirically. This is the case in all of your dissertation chapters. As Kumar (2011) argues:

> The *literature review* is an integral part of the research process and makes a valuable contribution to almost every operational step. It has value even before the first step; that is, when you are merely thinking about a research question that you may want to find answers to through your research journey. In the initial stages of research it helps you establish the theoretical roots of your study, clarify your ideas and develop your research methodology. Late in the process, the literature review serves to enhance and consolidate your own knowledge base and helps you to integrate your findings with the existing body of knowledge. Since an important responsibility in research is to compare your findings with those of others, it is here that the literature review plays an extremely important role. During the write-up … it helps you to integrate your findings with existing knowledge – that is, to either support or contradict earlier research. (2011: 31–2, original emphasis)

So, different types of literatures will do different sorts of work in your dissertation. In some cases you will use the literature to provide a theoretical background to your dissertation. How have others gone about theorizing the topic you are studying? Is there one theory that has become dominant? Or, are there a range of theories that co-exist, vying for dominance? In other cases the literature you cite and draw upon will allow you to compare your findings with those in other studies. So, you are studying the planning process in Oran. What do previous studies of the city in general and its planning in particular say? What about other studies within Algeria, or within the wider North African region?

A further body of literature will allow you to write in an informed manner about your choice of research methods. What sorts of methods have been used by studies answering similar research questions used? What sorts of knowledge do you want to generate? As you will see reading through the rest of this book, there are a number of methods used to study cities. Your choice of methods is one that needs to be made in relation to your philosophical and theoretical approaches, as all the authors in this collection explain. Each method has its advantages and disadvantages. It is particularly important that you learn from the work of others who have done research on your topic. So, if you decide you want to study housing markets in Latin American cities and the majority of work in this field uses pre-constructed secondary data on cost and tenure then you need to think about whether you want to do likewise, or to approach the topic slightly differently. That might mean asking a different set of questions of housing markets in Latin American cities, which would necessitate thinking about the research methods that might allow you to answer these questions. For example, and to quote Cloke et al. (2004: 37), 'We may want to know things about the characteristics, activities, worldviews, and the like of people living in a given locality.' If this is the case for you, then throughout this volume perhaps interviews (Cochrane, Chapter 4), ethnography (Swanson, Chapter 5), diaries (Latham, Chapter 8) or videos (Garrett, Chapter 10) might be most appropriate.

Perhaps the literature that students find hardest to use in their dissertations is that on different ways of knowing. '[P]hilosophies inform work and … research questions are always based on assumptions and choices between different ways of knowing', according to Aitken and Valentine (2006: 13). So, an important aspect of the formative work you do for your dissertation is to find out about the philosophical approaches adopted by others working on the same sorts of topics that you believe will form the cornerstone of your dissertation. This aspect of the dissertation is non-negotiable. As Kitchin and Tate (2000: 4) correctly state, 'no research … takes place in a philosophical vacuum'. Cities continue to be researched from a range of different philosophical perspectives. At any one time a particular approach may be dominant. Certainly much of the late 1970s/early 1980s urban studies literature was heavily informed by Marxism, and in particular the writings of Manuel Castells (1977) and David Harvey (1973), amongst others. This matters in terms of the research questions that were asked, the subjects or topics that were valued and studied, the methods that were used, and how the findings were written up. The current studying of cities is not dominated by any one approach. If you read urban studies textbooks, whether written out of anthropology, human geography, planning or sociology, that much should be clear (Davies and Imbroscio 2008, 2011; Gottdiener and Hutchison 2010; Low 1999; Pacione 2009). So, as you read the work of academics on the topic or topics you currently believe will constitute the focus of your dissertation, stop and think about their philosophical approach. Your choice is one that has to be made in relation to the kinds of theories and methods you intend to use in your dissertation, as if to reinforce how the different elements of the research process are all interconnected. It is not a choice that can be made in splendid isolation. Many of you will probably adopt a post-colonial or a post-structural approach. Be clear what this might mean for the topic you study, how you study it, and what you do with the data you generate. Others may adopt a positivist approach, and all that goes with it. There is no absolute 'right' or 'wrong' philosophical approach when you are thinking about studying cities. Rather, the goal should be for you to become familiar with the academic literature that exists on what you expect to be your dissertation topic and to understand the links between the theoretical, philosophical and methodological approaches adopted in this work.

Returning to Flick's (2011) different types of 'wider contexts', underpinning each of them is a set of assumptions that you know what you are looking for, which may or may not be the case. Hart (1998: 13) defines a literature review's content as:

> The selection of available documents (both published and unpublished) on the topic, which contain information, ideas, data, and evidence written from a particular standpoint to fulfil certain aims or express certain views on the nature of the topic and how it is to be investigated, and the effective evaluation of these documents in relation to the research being proposed.

Locating theoretical, methodological and empirical literature for your dissertation is an art not a science, however. While there are some systematic ways of going about searching, such as those outlined by Martin and Flowerdew (2005), ultimately you need to factor in some time spent that generates little by way of return. Or that is how it might seem. However, it is the act of searching and what you learn through the process, rather than what you do or do not find, that might ultimately benefit you most in your study. You are likely to hone your topic, focus your research questions, and generally rework your emphasis in and through searching for literature, in the process fixing more closely on what is and what is not 'relevant'. Taking notes on what you have found, reading theoretical pieces alongside one another, discussing the virtues of different methods, exploring possible case studies for your dissertation – this is the iterative work that you will do as you situate your dissertation. So, rather than a set of 'relevant' literatures – theoretical, methodological and empirical – waiting to be discovered by you, they are in fact constituted and reconstituted by the work you do. Until you have finished and submitted your dissertation it is not so easy to draw firm lines around 'relevant' and 'not relevant' literatures. Only through this situational work will you become clearer on the focus of your dissertation, your research questions and how you will go about addressing them.

Conclusion

This chapter has taken you quickly through the different elements of producing a dissertation up to the point where you begin to undertake research. It has emphasized the need to plan the dissertation as a project, with a clear timescale and milestones. There are risks involved in producing a dissertation, of which you need to be aware. An important element to producing a dissertation is your engagement with, and use of, existing literatures. There will be philosophical, theoretical, methodological and empirical literatures that you will need to discover, read, learn from and think about how you use in your own work: 'No writing is done in a vacuum' (Walliman 2011: 315). The different literatures will become more or less 'relevant' as you hone and refine your topic and research questions, something you do best through reading the work of others, whether it is a piece in a newspaper, an item on television or an article in an academic journal. All of us are 'largely dependent upon data for the successful completion of our research projects' (Cloke et al. 2004: 35), and the following eight chapters will each discuss a particular method, the type of data it generates and its use as part of an urban project.

References

Aitken, S. and Valentine, G. (2006) Philosophies, in S. Aitken and G. Valentine (eds), *Approaches to Human Geography*. London: Sage, pp. 13–19.
Castells, M. (1977) *The Urban Question*. Boston, MA: MIT Press.

Cloke, P., Cook, I., Goodwin, M., Painter, J. and Philo, C. (eds) (2004) *Practising Human Geography.* London: Sage.

Davies, J. and Imbroscio, D. (eds) (2008) *Theories of Urban Politics.* London: Sage.

Davies, J. and Imbroscio, D. (eds) (2011) *Critical Urban Studies.* London: Sage.

Flick, U. (2011) *Introducing Research Methodology: A Beginner's Guide to Doing a Research Project.* London: Sage.

Gatrell, A.C. and Flowerdew, R. (2005) Choosing a topic, in R. Flowerdew and D.M. Martin (eds) *Methods in Human Geography: A Guide for Students Doing a Research Project.* Harlow: Pearson Education, pp. 38–47.

Gottdiener, M. and Hutchison, R. (eds) (2010) *The New Urban Sociology* (4th edn). Boulder, CO: Westview Press.

Harrison, M. and Whalley, B. (2008) Understanding a dissertation from start to finish: the process and the product. *Journal of Geography in Higher Education,* 32: 401–18.

Hart, C. (1998) *Doing a Literature Review.* London: Sage.

Harvey, D. (1973) *Social Justice and the City.* Baltimore, MD: Johns Hopkins University Press.

Kennedy, B.A. (1999) First catch your hare … research designs for individual projects, in A. Rogers, H. Viles and A. Goudie (eds), *The Student's Companion to Geography.* Oxford: Blackwell, pp. 128–34.

Kitchin, R. and Tate, N. (2000) *Conducting Research into Human Geography: Theory, Methodology and Practice.* Harlow: Prentice Hall.

Kumar, R. (2011) *Research Methodology: A Step-By-Step Guide for Beginners.* London: Sage.

Low, S. (ed.) (1999) *Theorizing the City: The New Anthropology Reader.* Oxford: Blackwell.

Martin, D.M. and Flowerdew, R. (2005) Introduction, in R. Flowerdew and D.M. Martin (eds), *Methods in Human Geography: A Guide for Students Doing a Research Project.* Harlow: Pearson Education.

Pacione, M. (2009) *Urban Geography: A Global Perspective* (3rd edn). London: Routledge.

Ragin, C.C. (1994) *Constructing Social Research.* Thousand Oaks, CA: Pine Forge Press.

Smith, K., Todd, M. and Waldman, J. (2009) *Doing Your Undergraduate Social Science Dissertation.* London: Routledge.

Walliman, N. (2004) *Your Undergraduate Dissertation: The Essential Guide for Success.* London: Sage.

Walliman, N. (2011) *Your Research Project: Designing and Planning Your Work* (3rd edn). London: Sage.

3

ARCHIVAL RESEARCH

Stephen V. Ward

Introduction

An immense amount of source material for research about cities exists in archives. This chapter gives a brief overview of the opportunities for archival research on urban topics, highlighting how appropriate archive records can be located and used most effectively. Examples will be drawn largely from research into the historical development of urban planning. However, many issues are typical of other kinds of urban research topics. For example, the chapter highlights the nature of archival research compared to other research methods. It also shows how the research evidence from archive materials is not confined to their immediate content. More hidden meanings can be uncovered from the interpretation of documents prepared for quite different purposes. The chapter also discusses how archival research evidence can be incorporated into research projects such as undergraduate and graduate dissertations. Like the rest of the book, therefore, it is a practical guide that also raises bigger questions about methodology which you should consider before, during and after your research (see Chapter 2, this volume).

What are archives?

In most cases, archives are specialized buildings or parts of buildings such as libraries or museums where various kinds of records are kept and, in most cases, made available to researchers. Some archives are major national institutions, such as the UK National Archives at Kew in London (www.nationalarchives.gov.uk), which house the records of the state. There are equivalent institutions in most countries, normally based in capital cities, though in federal nations such as the United States of America (www.archives.gov/) or Australia (www.naa.gov.au/) actual records can usually be accessed elsewhere. Most countries also have other archives of national or sometimes wider significance. In the UK, for example, the archives of the Royal Institute of British Architects are housed within the Victoria and Albert Museum (www.vam.ac.uk/content/articles/v/vam-riba-collections). It contains the drawings and personal papers of many individuals who played important roles in shaping the face of cities.

Most affluent countries also have many sub-national archives. All federal nations have important state or provincial archives. Scotland also has its own national archives in Edinburgh. Below these there will usually be archive offices organized at regional or local level which hold many records of local and regional significance, including those of local and regional government and newspapers. In addition some have wider interest for broader research topics. In the UK, for example, the Hertfordshire County Archives house important records of the garden city and new towns movements (www.hertsdirect.org/services/leisculture/heritage1/hals).

Major universities also have diverse archive collections. The University of Liverpool in the UK, for example, has the papers of two very important British planners (who both worked extensively elsewhere), Lord Holford and Gordon Stephenson (http://sca.lib.liv.ac.uk/collections). In the USA, Cornell University holds the papers of the major American planner Clarence Stein (http://rmc.library.cornell.edu/ead/htmldocs/RMM03600.html) and the George Mason University in Virginia holds the valuable Planned Communities Archive (http://sca.gmu.edu/finding_aids/pca.html). In quite a different vein, the University of Sussex in the UK houses the archive of the Mass Observation social research organization (www.massobs.org.uk/overview_collections.htm). This includes many very detailed reports that together chronicle everyday life throughout Britain from 1937 to the early 1950s, indicating much about the daily practices, attitudes and opinions (including about planning) of ordinary people.

Many organizations will, of course, have closed archives relating to their current business. However some non-current historical records remain with their originating organizations, which make them available to researchers. On the whole such arrangements are more typical in the USA. The Columbia Archives in the privately developed planned new town of the same name in Maryland are one such example (www.columbiaarchives.org). As well as the archives of the new town itself, they also hold the records of its developer, James Rouse, an internationally significant innovator in several fields of urban development. In the UK many comparable records have been deposited in public archives or universities. However, many organizations retain their own archives. One such is the Town and Country Planning Association (originally the Garden City Association), which keeps its own archives covering its long history (Bassett 1980).

What kinds of record are in archives?

The typical records found in these different kinds of archives are text documents, which might be handwritten, typewritten or printed. Photographs, drawings and maps represent other kinds of archived records that are potentially significant for urban researchers. The common feature is that all are documents produced at a particular point in time to represent some activity, event, scene or set of circumstances for a specific purpose. The very words 'record' or 'document' have tended to signify what we now call a 'hard copy', that is, something produced on paper. Increasingly, however, more documents may for conservation or space reasons be made available to researchers in other forms, such as digitally or on microfilm. In recent years, more records have also been originated in a digital form.

Both these recent developments are beginning to stretch the notion of the archive from a collection of hard copy documents held in a specific building to something that exists virtually, capable of being accessed remotely. In a few cases, for example Historic Digimap, many older maps published by the British Ordnance Survey can now be accessed electronically (http://edina.ac.uk/digimap/description/historic_overview.shtml). This is also increasingly the case for many local photographic archives. The UK National Archives has recently begun to implement a policy for archiving websites and other digital media, which opens further possibilities for research (www.nationalarchives.gov.uk/information-management/projects-and-work/digital-preservation.htm). More ambitiously, the US National Archives and Records Administration is presently working in partnership with Google to digitize its entire collections. It seems likely this trend will in time become much more widespread.

Planning archival research

What records are likely to be available?

Each research approach offers opportunities but will also constrain the scope and form of your research. Unlike most other forms of research, archival work is self-evidently limited to events and phenomena for which records, mainly written, have already been made. It is also clearly more appropriate for research with a historical dimension. But what does 'historical' actually mean in this context? Almost always there is some delay before documents become available for archival research. Private organizations (including privatized companies formerly in public ownership) or individuals are entirely free to release or withhold their records as they see fit. Many will actually release at least some of their records but when, where and how is their choice.

Regarding records created by government and public bodies in democratic countries, two important principles shape when and to what extent researchers can inspect such records. The first is that citizens of democratic countries should be able by right to inspect public documents on request unless there are specific reasons (for example, security, commercial or personal) to withhold them. The second is that individuals should have a right of privacy over information collected about them.

The varied interplay of these principles has produced different practices in different countries. The US system (and that of Canada) is based on open access. In theory all public documents can be requested, although in practice there are many exceptions. In the UK (along with Australia and Ireland) most retained documents are released after a specified period. In the UK this is currently 30 years, now (2013–18) being progressively reduced to 20. However, certain records, mainly personal or security files, are retained for longer periods. To further complicate the position, this approach has been modified, as in many other countries, by freedom-of-information legislation. This has gone some way to open access on request, releasing many very recent documents and some that were formerly retained beyond 30 years (Dacre 2009: 6–8).

What does (and doesn't) survive?

Despite these various (albeit shrinking) restrictions, vast quantities of material, often covering the relatively recent past, can be found in archives. Yet even these are far from being all that were ever produced on their respective subjects. Only a small proportion is actually retained. The UK National Archives, for example, keep only the approximately 5 per cent of public records that are judged as having enduring historical value. The US National Archives and Research Administration retains only between 1 and 3 per cent of federal government documents in perpetuity.

In other cases, important records may have been wilfully or accidentally destroyed or lost prior to collections ending up in proper archives. This sad fate befell many of the papers of Sir Ebenezer Howard, a key figure in modern urban planning. At least, though, what survived did eventually end up in a suitable archive (Hertfordshire). At present there are collections of planning-related records in many countries which lack a suitable archival home. A key reason is often that such collections, typically of deceased prominent individuals in planning or defunct organizations, are neither well organized nor clearly catalogued. They may be held by well-meaning individuals, often family members or those intending to write books, but the long-term effects of keeping papers in lofts, sheds or garages are often unfortunate. The misfortunes of life also mean that the papers may come into the hands of others who do not value their significance.

The other side of this problem is that public archives often lack the space, funds or human resources to organize new acquisitions. Often some kind of dowry or grant is needed to underwrite the cost of their successful integration. Even some collections that are in archives often remain only partially organized. Catalogues (especially those accessible on the WorldWide Web) may also be sketchy or incomplete. You will have to learn to 'read between the lines' of catalogue entries to decide what documents to request.

Preparing for archival research

How then can you respond to this often bewildering picture and find suitable archival material? For many modest research projects with a clear locational focus, the relevant local or regional archives will be the obvious starting point. Yet, even in such cases, other archives may be relevant. Decisions about important local government policies, for example, especially controversial ones, will often have been considered at national level, with records created and hopefully retained as a result. The involvement of national pressure groups adds another dimension that may have generated material in other archives. And, of course, many more ambitious research projects will not be confined to one locality.

For such projects, the web, despite any imperfections at a more detailed level, certainly helps researchers to locate relevant archives. For UK researchers the National Archives website (www.nationalarchives.gov.uk) provides an access point for all kinds of archives, not just the national public records that it holds. Very importantly, it also hosts the Archon gateway which identifies and locates many publicly accessible archives around the world (www.nationalarchives.gov.uk/archon/). Although this website's advice is specific to the UK, the same pattern of access is reproduced in many other countries, respective national archives also serving as gateways. There are also other important web gateways, which vary greatly from country to country. In Canada, for example, www.archivescanada.ca gives access to the catalogues of all the country's major archives. The Archives Hub (http://archiveshub.ac.uk/) is another important resource, mainly concerned with archives held in UK universities. Finally we can note the important resource on non-governmental organizations and pressure groups operating in the UK since 1945 (www.dango.bham.ac.uk/index.htm). The records of these types of organizations are notoriously difficult to track down, so this recently created database is particularly welcome.

The need for direct contact

When you have got the scent of likely archives, it is best to make direct contact with archivists there. Almost invariably they will be helpful as to how collections can most successfully be used. Obviously, though, this will depend on how clear you are about what you wish to investigate. In some cases archivists may be extremely knowledgeable about the detailed contents of their collections but this does not mean they can or should define what your investigation should be about. They may well, however, know of previous research work on the specific collections. This itself can give you additional contacts who may be able to advise how best to use the resource. Before you can do this, however, you must have one or more clear research questions which put some clear limits on the scale of the intended work (see Chapter 2, this volume).

Once you have a broad plan for research in a particular archive, it is essential to make an appointment with the archivist about the timing of a visit and what documents are required. In very large archives, such as the UK National Archives, an automatic document pre-ordering system is available via the Internet. Apart from the details of the actual research, various practical arrangements for access can also be checked. The opening times of archives can be quite short, often significantly less than those of libraries. Some archives require users to become members. Usually (but not invariably) this and actual use of the archives are free but researchers, especially students, may need suitable identification and possibly a reference from, for example, their host institution or adviser/supervisor to verify that they can be trusted to use the records properly.

Other considerations are what arrangements exist for taking notes. Laptop use is now widely presumed but some smaller archives will only have a limited number of workspaces. Many archives do not allow pens to be used and some will not even allow them (or rubbers or pencil sharpeners) to be taken into rooms where documents are produced. The arrangements for copying documents should also be checked. Eventually, digitization projects will reduce the significance of this. Photocopying in archives can be expensive because of the care needed with sometimes fragile documents. However a very welcome recent development is the growing freedom to use digital cameras, which put documents at much less risk. By no means do all archives currently permit photography and some will make a charge but this is usually worth it. You can save time and money by this means, especially in archives distant from your home. If any more than a few records are photographed, however, the images should be carefully sorted and (probably) printed out immediately after a visit to archives if they are to be comprehensible for use in your dissertation.

Doing archival research

Reading archival records critically

The key thing to remember when undertaking archival research is that the material being examined was prepared for purposes other than your project. This way of gathering evidence differs from other forms of research where the raw material is directly researcher-generated. In archival work, you are essentially interpreting and deriving meaning from other people's representations of various sets of circumstances (Scott 1990: esp. 28–35). If the research question invites only a descriptive answer, for example about the unfolding of events, archival research may simply involve finding the appropriate records and summarizing them. But if some deeper problematic is being explored (as it usually is in any worthwhile piece of work), then you will need to approach that question indirectly in your reading of archival records. A key skill of archival research is knowing how to do this.

Any record can be considered to encompass at least two and perhaps more levels of discourse and therefore research meaning. The primary discourse of any record is concerned with the specific things that it documents – for example, that a particular set of people were present and caused something to happen on a particular date in a particular place. The most obvious aspects of a record's secondary discourse would be concerned with matters of immediate context: why were these people there, who were they and what prior knowledge and ideologies did they bring to the event? Beyond that, there would be the wider context: how far were the actions they were taking being shaped by individuals or forces that were not directly recorded?

In order to derive and explore these different levels of meaning, you must always consider why any archival records being used were originally prepared and by (and for) whom. Were they part of an ongoing process or did they record some end point where a decision was reached or something else significant was recorded as having happened? What kind of 'language' is used in preparing the record – does it, for example, represent some kind of 'insider discourse' where highly specialist terms are used or does it use more accessible, everyday language? Would the document when it was originally prepared have been widely accessible, or was its circulation likely to have been confined to a few people and if so who and why? Whose 'voices' are present in the record and whose are not? What are the document's 'silences', the matters ignored or marginalized? As these questions are addressed, it becomes possible to understand the ideologies that shaped the formation of the record and the point of view that it embodies.

For many researchers, these critical skills develop with experience as ever-larger numbers of archival records are inspected and interrogated. Yet it is inherently more difficult to achieve this if you are confined to one set of records originating from a single source (for example a central government ministry or a local authority). It is easy, particularly when examining a large number of such documents, to begin to accept without question the scheme of representation adopted by the authors of the document. However, it is very important that you are able to look beyond this and maintain a critical distance.

Examining different sources

As in any other forms of research, a key way of doing this is to examine other sources on the same subject. Accounts by other researchers based on their own research may help you to do this. In a bigger research project, however, this would probably involve the use of other original sources. Often the most convenient way of doing this is to look for contemporary comment in newspapers (or in other media, for example from the BBC written archives). This is not to say that the media should be regarded as the last word on matters of accuracy or objectivity. But they will often highlight tensions or controversies and give a voice to interests on which more official documents may be silent. The historic archives of major newspapers can now be accessed online (often free to students going through their institutions' libraries) with usually excellent subject search facilities. The local press is still less easy to use but dates of key events often provide pointers as to where to begin searching. Press-cuttings collections accumulated by public agencies can also be invaluable and sometimes appear in official record files.

If you are very lucky, there may also be personal archives or memoirs of key actors involved. These can give a different and often more vivid perspective, perhaps revealing sides to the story different to that which emerges from purely official sources. If they exist, such sources often show that, alongside the official process of committees, minutes and formal letters, there are often important personal interchanges occurring away from formal arenas. The well known (published) diaries of Richard Crossman, who was a government minister of housing, planning and local government in the 1960s, are a case in point (Crossman 1975). Still more revealing were the earlier diaries of Berthold Lubetkin, the architect/planner of the abortive but widely celebrated and highly radical plan for the coal mining New Town of Peterlee in County Durham during 1948—50 (RIBA Archives, LUB/15/20). And there are others becoming available, sometimes on the web.

How much is enough?

As these other avenues for research suggest themselves, what initially may have seemed a manageable programme of archival work can soon start to burgeon, causing anxiety for researchers. This is compounded by stories that every experienced archival researcher can tell about how they made important discoveries by accident. For example, it was only the arrival of a mistakenly ordered file from the early 1950s about the New Towns that led the official historian, the late Barry Cullingworth, to discover that the Conservative government at the time was actively considering scrapping the whole programme (Cullingworth 1979). Other cases include the finding of key items in places quite unsuspected from their catalogue descriptions. The long unpublished report of the distinguished British planner Colin Buchanan's 1962 visit to the United States when preparing his seminal *Traffic in Towns* report turned up in this way (UK National Archives, HLG 136/49; Ward 2007: 380–1).

Such moments of discovery can seem little short of sublime, at least amongst the sort of people who enjoy working in the archives. The desire for such highs can, though, have a strangely addictive quality. And, like every addiction, it has a downside. Fear of missing some great discovery can result in excessive prolongation of a research project. All programmes of work in the archives must therefore have some exit strategy. A clear plan of investigation should involve a specified list of documents, an element of sampling of documents that seem as if they may have some relevance, and some flexibility to allow unexpected trails discovered en route to be followed. But then, move on. In archival as other forms of investigation, research is an attitude of mind that may well persist for life but for most researchers it has to be delivered in the form of finite programmes. As a student you will have a deadline and in most cases this will be non-negotiable. However fascinating the archival work you are doing, a missed submission will incur serious penalties!

Writing up archival research

Not overdoing it

Great discipline is also needed in writing up archival work. You will almost certainly have a word limit beyond which you cannot go. There is a big temptation to parade much more of the detailed evidence than is really necessary to develop the argument. Anyone who reads novels will probably have come across authors who cannot resist parading the fruits of their research across many tedious pages quite unnecessary for the development of the plot. Their equivalent in dissertations are those of you who find yourselves unable to refrain from larding your accounts with great slabs of verbatim quotations, often of banal details or rhetorical flourishes that could much more succinctly be expressed in your own words.

Quotations can certainly give an authentic feel to the research but the researcher should be aware how quickly the returns diminish with excessive use. They should be used mainly to highlight key phrases that reveal the processes and perceptions which are evident in the documents. If longer quotations are necessary, they should be used selectively, perhaps to illustrate an example of a more general phenomenon rather than documenting all possible instances. References should always be included to show the researcher has done the work and to allow others to follow up in their own way. (There are usually conventional ways of citing from particular archives so that the precise location of evidence can be clearly specified.) But the effect to be aimed for is that of a researcher who is in command of the evidence but not overwhelmed by it.

Jumping easily from an extensive body of very detailed notes to the desired succinct account that combines a strong sense of narrative direction with sharp and vivid insights into the larger themes of the research is not easily done. Many researchers find it useful after a spell in the archives to reflect on the way their findings are shaping up, writing summaries, noting what seem to be critical episodes that might be given prominence in the final version. These might be discussed with supervisors, fellow students or (sparingly so as not to strain tolerance) parents or partners. Regular articulation of your emergent understanding of your research topic is a good way of working out what the final version that you will submit needs to say. It will also help you to find the right words and expressions to do it succinctly and effectively.

Integrating archival findings with other evidence

In the final write up, archival evidence will often be integrated with that gathered in other ways. Clearly other methods may generate their own write-up needs. However, seen from the perspective of archival research, it is usually preferable to integrate these other sources of evidence as much as possible. This allows the possibilities of documentary research to be more effectively demonstrated (and its limitations moderated).

A common way in which this integration can occur is that interim documents concerned with the evolution of thought or policy are compared with a final published version. Sir Ebenezer Howard's archive, for example, contains earlier drafts of his famous 1898 book *To-Morrow: A Peaceful Path to Real Reform* which set out his vision of the garden city (Ward 2002). Comparison of these with the published version reveals underlying political values that he subsequently camouflaged to widen the book's appeal. His famous three-magnets diagram, for example, originally incorporated the word 'socialism', replaced in the published version by the less contentious 'co-operation'. Another diagram lost its Messianic slogan 'Go up and possess the land!' in the published version.

Another common kind of integration would be of personal interview material either derived directly by the researcher or increasingly from oral history projects. Such approaches can be important to fill in gaps in the sometimes bare details of official reports. They can also help to assess the impacts of planned environments in use by integrating the perspectives of those people underrepresented in documentary archives. The 'planned for' who live their lives in the towns and cities that planners and political leaders aspire to shape have often been neglected in accounts relying on official records. There has been a growing tendency to integrate oral history methods into studies of, for example, post-war reconstruction of bombed cities or New Town development (e.g. Hubbard et al. 2003; Llewellyn 2004). Interviews with key actors are also often a better way to get a fuller sense of more creative processes. These were rarely adequately written down in documents until they were in an advanced state. Gordon Stephenson, the former head of Planning Technique at the Ministry of Town and Country Planning during the most formative years of the 1940s, disarmingly admitted to an interviewer in 1992 that he and his colleagues deliberately kept their discussions off file until they had decided what to do (see Ward 2012). They are sobering words for any researcher, not to put all his or her faith in archives.

Conclusion

No methods are perfect, of course. Despite the various health warnings made in this chapter, archival research remains the only way of gathering extensive detailed research evidence that was compiled at the time. It is particularly suitable for research with a historical dimension but is a skill that all researchers ought to possess to some extent. Even if used only in a supporting role alongside other methods, archival research can garner results of unique value and authority. Mastery of archival sources and their use in research can often be prized as a sign of true scholarship. Yet care is needed in using archives. Unlike research methods where evidence is directly generated by the researcher, a key part of archival work is finding out if suitable material exists, where it is and whether it is accessible. Persistence is sometimes needed, especially where archives are not well catalogued. But the archival quest does not end when these matters are overcome.

Once found, it is important always to appreciate that the archival materials were generated for purposes other than your particular project. Depending on why they were compiled, by whom and for what purpose, they will have strengths and weaknesses as sources of information and understanding. If the full value of an archival source is to be realized, these aspects must be recognized. Archival texts need to be read and interpreted at levels deeper than face value, with supplementary work as necessary to reveal their surrounding contextual dimensions. Many archival records are compiled by people or organizations with sufficient resources, organization and power to make and maintain records. This will inevitably have an impact on the way the circumstances dealt with in the documents are represented. The voices of some interests may well be excluded or detectable only in a muted form. Sometimes, however, this limitation can be offset by using other archival sources or by other research methods, such as those discussed in other chapters.

All these things mean that archival research can be difficult to confine within predefined limits. As on-going relaxations in document release occur and digital access increases the quantum of new archival material, this challenge to researchers will also grow. But the possibilities will surely outweigh these challenges. Whether in traditional archives or virtually at a remote computer or other electronic device, researchers will soon be able to reap the full rewards of the information revolution of recent decades. The opportunities it presents for researchers of all kinds will be immense. Students preparing dissertations can certainly share these. Never before has the scope to use such a wide range of rich research material in archives been so great.

Frequently Asked Questions

1. How could I locate records appropriate to my research?

If your research focuses on a particular area, contact the local archive office. If the focus is national or international, use the appropriate national archives website either directly to identify appropriate records or locate other relevant archives.

2. What do I need to consider in preparing for my work in the archives?

Before your first visit, make an appointment and check what will be needed from you, what the rules are about computers, cameras, pens, etc. Every time you visit, pre-order as precisely as possible the records you wish to examine.

3. How can I read archival materials critically?

Establish why and by whom the documents you are examining were prepared. Find out as much as you can about the individuals, institutions and processes which are recorded. Ask yourself whose interests are absent from the documents, and why.

4. How can I offset any limitations in the archival sources I am using?

Examine other records that report or comment on the same subject (for example, newspapers or other mass media). If possible, conduct your own interviews with individuals involved or affected. Seek relevant secondary accounts.

5. How can I distil my research notes into a cogent final account?

Regularly review your notes and consider how they relate to your main research questions. Discuss your evolving thinking with your supervisor/adviser. Produce a full draft of the relevant sections of your research soon after your archival work is complete.

Follow Up References

Scott, J. (1990) *A Matter of Record: Documentary Sources in Social Research.* Cambridge: Polity Press.

This very thorough account by a sociologist considers different types of documents, including those that were one-off records and those of a more routine, repetitive nature. It is especially insightful about the problems that arise in deriving research meaning from documents.

Hoggart, K., Lees, L. and Davies, A. (2002) *Researching Human Geography*. London: Arnold.

Chapter 4 of this book gives a fuller account than the present chapter of the practicalities and methodological issues involved in documentary research. It is especially useful for geographical and related research giving specific urban examples. The examples show how detailed documents can be used to research urban change.

Prior, L. (2003) *Using Documents in Social Research*. London: Sage.

This provides an interesting contrast with the present chapter. It discusses how to use less-formal types of documents, such as those prepared as part of professional employment or other purposes on a short-term, working basis which may not necessarily ever be housed in archives.

www.archivesmadeeasy.org

This website, hosted by the London School of Economics, focuses on international history. However, the helpful information and practical advice it contains is of interest to other researchers. The so-called 'easy archives tips' help researchers prepare for work in specific major archives around the world.

www.nationalarchives.gov.uk/archon

There are many published or semi-published guides to archive collections. Increasingly material of this kind is web-available or web-created. This particular resource can guide researchers to many publicly accessible collections throughout the world. It is also accessible through the national archive websites of many other countries.

References

Bassett, P. (1980) A list of the historical records of the Town and Country Planning Association, Birmingham/Reading: Centre of Urban and Regional Studies, University of Birmingham/Institute of Agricultural History, University of Reading, GB2276 TCPA, digitised by the National Archives.

Crossman, R.H.S. (1975) *The Diaries of a Cabinet Minister, Vol. 1: Minister of Housing 1964–66*. London: Hamish Hamilton.

Cullingworth, J.B. (1979) *Environmental Planning, 1939–1969, Vol. III: New Towns Policy*. London: HMSO.

Dacre, P. (Chairman) (2009) *Review of the 30 Year Rule*. Norwich: The Stationery Office.

Hubbard, P., Faire, L. and Lilley, K. (2003) Contesting the modern city: reconstruction and everyday life in post-war Coventry. *Planning Perspectives*, 18: 377–97.

Llewellyn, M. (2004) Producing and experiencing Harlow: neighbourhood units and narratives. *Planning Perspectives*, 19: 155–74.

RIBA Archives, LUB/15/20. Archives of Berthold Lubetkin, RIBA Collection, Victoria and Albert Museum, London.

Scott, J. (1990) *A Matter of Record: Documentary Sources in Social Research*. Cambridge: Polity Press.

UK National Archives, HLG 136/49, Buchanan Unit: Setting up of the Crowther Steering Group, Visit to America – Report by C.D. Buchanan 1962.

Ward, S.V. (2002) Ebenezer Howard: His life and times, in K.C. Parsons and D. Schuyler (eds), *From Garden City to Green City: The Legacy of Ebenezer Howard*. Baltimore, MD: Johns Hopkins University Press, pp. 14–37.

Ward, S.V. (2007) Cross-national learning in the formation of British planning policies 1940–99: a comparison of the Barlow, Buchanan and Rogers Reports. *Town Planning Review*, 78: 369–400.

Ward, S.V. (2012) Gordon Stephenson and the 'galaxy of talent': planning for post-war reconstruction in Britain 1942–1947. *Town Planning Review*, 83: 279–96.

Websites

<www.archives.gov> US National Archives and Records Administration

<http://archiveshub.ac.uk> The Archives Hub

<www.archivescanada.ca> Archives Canada

<www.columbiaarchives.org> Columbia Archives

<www.dango.bham.ac.uk/index.htm> Database of Archives of Non-Governmental Organisations

<http://edina.ac.uk/digimap/description/historic_overview.shtml> Historic Digimap

<www.hertsdirect.org/services/leisculture/heritage1/hals> Hertfordshire County Archives

<www.massobs.org.uk/overview_collections.htm> The Mass Observation Archive, University of Sussex

<www.naa.gov.au> National Archives of Australia

<www.nationalarchives.gov.uk> UK National Archives

<http://rmc.library.cornell.edu/ead/htmldocs/RMM03600.html> Clarence Stein Papers, Division of Rare and Manuscript Collections, Cornell University Library

<http://sca.gmu.edu/finding_aids/pca.html> Planned Communities Archives, Special Collections and Archives, George Mason University

<http://sca.lib.liv.ac.uk/collections> University of Liverpool Library Special Collections and Archives

<www.vam.ac.uk/content/articles/v/vam-riba-collections> Victoria and Albert Museum – Royal Institute of British Architects Collection

4

INTERVIEWS

Allan Cochrane

Introduction

Two main strands can be identified in (sometimes productive) tension between each other when it comes to researching the city: the first is largely focused on the experience of everyday life – how people live their lives in the city; the second is more explicitly focused on charting sets of power relations within and beyond the city. It would be wrong to imply that there is some unbridgeable divide between these two sets of concerns but it would be equally mistaken to pretend that there are no differences in emphasis (and sometimes more). The aim in what follows in this chapter is not to present stark contrasts that make it necessary to choose between different epistemologies from the start, but rather to set out possibilities and explore ways of thinking through the implications of the choices that are made as part of the research process (from the questions that are asked to the research methods adopted and the answers that may be generated, see Chapter 2, this volume), as well as highlighting those areas in which there may be consistencies in approach across apparently disparate fields.

The interview is perhaps the most taken-for-granted social research method that there is, incorporated into the familiar ways in which people learn to interpret the social world as much as in the fieldwork practices of human geographers (e.g. see Cloke et al. 2004). It is ubiquitous as a technique in radio and television news and documentaries, with particular proponents of the art being praised for their forensic ability to extract confessions from the most recalcitrant of politicians, even as others are criticised for giving their subjects an easy ride. The interview is the basis of a whole array of journalistic practices. Most of us also have experience of being interviewed, for jobs or places on particular courses, whose purpose is to clarify our suitability for appointment or for a particular path of study (even if for those of us on the wrong side of the desk it sometimes appears to be little more than an exercise in ritual humiliation). Meanwhile, the police interview is also familiar, not only to those of us who have had the misfortune to have been called on to 'help the police with their enquiries', but also to anyone who has watched a cop show on television. And, of course, interviewing is a defining characteristic of work undertaken by a whole series of welfare professions, particularly associated with individual and family case work, including social work and health visiting, but also with a wider range of activities often associated with the prefix 'psy-', including counselling, therapy and psychoanalysis.

These days it would be hard to find many pieces of social science research seeking to understand the ways that cities work, whether as sites of day-to-day living or as spaces of political, social or economic power, that do not draw on interviews as at least one important source of evidence. Think about any piece with which you are familiar, and the evidence that is mobilized to make the argument. But in a way it is the very ubiquity of interviewing as a technique that we are all accustomed to using, or have seen used as a means of managing social life, that highlights the challenge of using it effectively as a research tool. There is a strong temptation to see the interview unproblematically as a means of uncovering truth, whether by exposing those we are interviewing (uncovering what they are hiding) or by acting as a conduit for them to express their views, by giving a voice to outsiders or acting as an insider reporting the views of the powerful or the rich (the people who are not like us) to an expectant world. Easy familiarity should always set off alarm bells for anyone seeking to engage in social research – it is important to reflect on the social relations that may already be entangled within any research method on which we draw.

In other words, rather than simply being a means of uncovering some underlying truth, the interview has to be understood as part of the process by which contemporary society is defined and individuals understand their position within it. As well as being a tool that is frequently utilised in the practice of social science research, and in researching cities in particular, the interview process is itself a social practice that requires examination (see e.g. Gubrium and Holstein 2002; Silverman 2004).

Historically – as Mike Savage (2010) powerfully reminds us – the interview has been distrusted by social scientists, largely because it is understood to be a performance, by interviewer and by interviewee. Instead there was greater reliance on observation, participation, immersion, involvement in 'natural' conversation – the aim (implicitly or explicitly) was to find some way of accessing behaviour and of 'listening in' on unselfconscious interaction that was somehow unsullied by the research process itself. At the other extreme, the formality of research was emphasized, finding an expression in the form of questionnaire surveys largely relying on closed questions of one sort or another; the systematic aggregation of data in this way was assumed to make it more susceptible to scientific – or at any rate mathematical – analysis.

The use of the interview as a research method has attracted criticism for what is identified as an underlying romanticism because of the way in which it implies or assumes that the interview offers a means of allowing people to reveal themselves as part of a search for some sort of authenticity (Gubrium and Holstein 2002: 13; Hammersley 2008: 89). However, the observational tradition can itself be criticized for incorporating its own form of romanticism – nothing is ever quite as neutral or 'natural' as such an approach implies and the problem of 'performance' by researcher as well as researched remains a real one, to the extent that it can sometimes feel as if the main focus is on allowing researchers to celebrate their own privileged access to (and sympathetic understanding of) some exoticized or problematized urban sub-culture.

And while the survey approach may be effective in identifying broader trends, it is less likely to be able to explain them or explore how they are understood by those experiencing or shaping them. So, rather than seeing the performative nature of the interview, and the extent to which the interview is a relationship between those involved in it (those constituted as interviewer and interviewee) as a means of ending the matter, it becomes necessary, rather, to take account of it in developing an approach to interviewing. As Martyn Hammersley (2008: 98) puts it, 'the fact that interviews are a distinctive type of situation does not necessarily mean that what happens in them carries no reliable implications about people's attitudes, perspectives etc.'

In this context, therefore, of critical engagement, it may first be worth just asking how researchers use interviews, and what they are expected to deliver.

What are interviews for?

Savage (2010) identifies two main interview traditions in the social sciences: the first was already being pursued by Sidney and Beatrice Webb in the early years of the twentieth century as they set out to find ways of understanding the structures of social relations and develop their own brand of socially progressive research. The Webbs both helped to generate a peculiarly British version of social democracy (characterized as Fabianism), which influenced the development of the Labour Party, and to define a particular approach to social research, which was initially given institutional form in the shape of the London School of Economics, which they helped to found. For them, the task was identified as being to talk to important (or knowledgeable) people and elicit information from them (about what they do, about their relationship to others, about their ways of working, their position in networks of power, about what they know as a result of their particular expertise or area of responsibility). Paul Cloke and others (Cloke et al. 2004: 123–4) set out the ways in which similar sets of understanding and similar approaches played a central part in the history of fieldwork approaches in human geography. The person being interviewed, in other words, is understood to be a provider of data – even a 'surrogate researcher' (Hammersley 2008: 91).

The second tradition is more concerned to find ways of allowing people to speak for themselves – to encourage them to discuss their own experiences and reflect on their understanding of them. The focus is on enabling people to express what they want to say and to find some way of understanding it. In other words, the aim is to allow (and even encourage) them to justify themselves, and express their own understanding of their role, their social position as well as their personal feelings. In this context, Paul Cloke and his co-authors helpfully define interviews as conversations with a purpose and explain that '[i]ntersubjective conversations with a purpose involve an active collusion between participants' (Cloke et al. 2004: 155).

Emphasis is often placed on relations, emotions and affect and with the particularities of power as it is produced through a range of practices rather than the uncovering of pre-existing structures of power and influence (see Pile 1991; Smith 2006). The importance of recognizing the interview as a relationship between interviewer and interviewee, jointly producing knowledge, is fundamental here. And understanding the interview as relationship means moving away from an approach that sees the role of the interviewer as being to extract knowledge, information or even meanings from the person being interviewed. Liz Bondi (2005: 443) draws directly on psychotherapeutic approaches to highlight the relational nature of the process – the 'betweenness of emotion' in the interview as 'a situated account of meaning-making and knowledge production'.

In the end, however, it would be a mistake to draw too clear a divide between these two ways of understanding the interview method. In a sense the second is also a reminder to those engaged in the first sort of interviewing (interviewing elites, professionals, policy actors) that they too need to think about the interview process itself – it is not enough simply to see it as a more or less neutral mechanism through which power relations can be identified and explored. Whatever the context and whatever the focus of the research, interviews need to be understood as relationships between interviewer and interviewee. As Sarah Neal and Eugene McLaughlin (2009) remind us, the work of policy elites may also involve significant emotional labour, which means that an approach that (for the purposes of research) somehow places them in a carefully bounded (antiseptic) category of their own is likely to be unhelpful.

Undertaking interviews with those already identified as powerful or defined as elites raises important questions. Katherine Smith (2006) strongly argues that it is misleading to start by assuming or identifying any group of people or individual as powerful as if it were a more or less necessary function of their position within some set of social, economic or political structures – instead it may be better to see power as something that is negotiated or assembled rather than something pre-existing just waiting to be called into play (see also Allen 2003). If this is the starting point, then interviews can be used to open up these processes, following up how the relationships are understood by a range of people being interviewed, without assuming any single interview delivers a straightforward answer to the question being explored.

But, of course, interviews are also used by researchers who view power rather differently, whether by those who see it as deeply rooted in structures of social and economic inequality, by those who come from a pluralist tradition that seeks to identify the relationship between interest groups of one sort or another, or by those who see it as still more elusive, expressed through networks of one sort or another (Judge et al. 1995).

Asking questions of those in power may also help in identifying unequal processes of decision making that benefit some at the expense of others, and in that context the first tradition with its focus on power and influence (which implies a continued distance between researcher and researched) remains an important one (see e.g. Cochrane 1998; Peck and Theodore 2012; Ward and Jones 1999). Building on his experience of researching Cardiff Bay's Urban Development Corporation in the 1990s, Mike Raco makes a powerful argument for the role that academic researchers might have in opening up powerful institutions to interrogation by more community-based organizations (Raco 1999). From a different perspective, in his exploration of the failure of a major urban transportation initiative, Bruno Latour combines a systematic approach to interviewing a series of significant human actors (policy professionals, technical experts, politicians, business people) with a review of policy and technical documents in ways that are intended to allow the voices of other (non-human) actors – such as the mechanisms to be integrated into the automatic systems – to be heard (Latour 1996).

The point here is not to dismiss one or other approach but to recognize the tensions between them and to think carefully about the ways in which interviews may help to inform research that has quite different starting points. How the interview process is approached will vary, depending on the philosophical or theoretical starting point and depending on the questions being asked; and, of course, the former will help to determine what questions are deemed to be worthwhile or helpful. Questions are generated from within not outside particular paradigms (or worldviews), however much effort is directed towards allowing the evidence to speak for itself.

What is an interview?

Thinking about these issues also necessarily raises the question of what an interview is. Not only is each interview different because each involves a particular relationship between interviewer and interviewee, researcher and researched, but more prosaically the form the interview takes may be chosen from a range that stretches from what has been called free association narrative (Hollway and Jefferson 2000) or open-ended (conversational) approaches, with little predetermined structure; to semi-structured interviews, often accompanied by an interview schedule with prompts of one sort or another; all the way (in principle at least) to highly structured formats inviting closed responses (for example, as undertaken as part of opinion polling). In what follows, the focus will be on the first two of these, since surveys are dealt with by Nik Theodore in Chapter 6 of this volume.

These more open-ended approaches are the ones most directly influenced by psychotherapeutic sets of understanding referred to above, and are largely concerned with understanding and exploring the meanings given by people to the lives that they lead and the relationships of which they are a part. Within a very broadly framed set of concerns, the aim is effectively to allow and even encourage the person being interviewed to talk, to express their own concerns and develop their own interpretations. This does not mean that the research is unfocused or the discussions simply range across subjects in an uncontrolled fashion – on the contrary, it requires researcher and researched to work together to explore a shared set of concerns. So, for example, in their book on free association and the interview method, Wendy Hollway and Tony Jefferson (2000) retain a focus on understanding and researching the fear of crime, drawing on the psychosocial subject to understand the relationship between the individual and her/his social positioning in terms of discourses, intersubjective relations and responses to events.

Liz Bondi (2003: 72) explores the interview relationship with the help of the notion of empathy – 'Imaginatively entering into another person's experiential world at the same time as retaining awareness of the difference between one's own unconscious experience and that of the other means being an observer of the process at the same time as being a participant.' The 'oscillation between observation and participation' that Bondi (2003: 72) highlights powerfully captures the experience of the interview as social science method, whatever the context. It is not possible to pretend that the interviewer is some sort of objective and distanced agent, divorced from the relationship of which she or he is a part, but it is nevertheless important to recognize that (however empathetic) the interviewer and interviewee are not reflecting on the same experiences, and in many cases the social distance between the two may be very wide (whether because the researcher is exploring the politics and lifestyles of the elite or those of the poor, across class, gender and ethnicity). Maintaining a separation is an important aspect of the process, allowing the researcher to interrogate and reflect on what is being said and how it is being said, without simply reproducing it.

In this context, too, it is important to recognize that interviews are not merely about the words that are spoken but also about a whole series of other interactions. It is not always possible to capture these effectively, but the challenge is to be aware of them – again the 'oscillation between observation and participation' is crucial, and the challenge is to be aware of it – to manage it consciously, rather than simply engage in it, as one might do in any more informal conversational setting. At its simplest, this may involve noting expressions, pauses or shifts in attitude, and systematic research notes can be as revealing as the recorded words. Mike Savage's (2010: 165–86) review of a series of interview-based projects dating back to the 1950s, drawing on the notes prepared at the time, provides fascinating insights into the relationship between researcher and researched at different times and different contexts as, for example, interviewers negotiate around domestic space and within households – highlighting the ways in which the research process both helps to frame how that space is understood and is itself framed by it.

If the open-ended approach to interviewing helps to deliver important insights into ways of understanding and managing the interview process, it is the semi-structured interview that seems to be dominant in qualitative research in human geography and city-focused research in particular. In part this may be because it might give you (not always justified) reassurance that you are in some sort of control and can direct the questions more or less effectively. This may be reinforced by the careful use of prompts – making it possible to follow up on points, ensuring that the broad direction of the questions is maintained. In practice, the division between open-ended (or free association) and semi-structured interviewing may be exaggerated, since a topic list will also be used even in the most open-ended of approaches, and the most effective semi-structured interviewing will necessarily encourage those being interviewed to reflect widely on the questions.

Nevertheless, the difference in emphasis is a real one and also reflects the distinction made above between research whose main purpose is to elicit information and chart networks of power and those whose main purpose is to explore meanings and sets of understanding. The semi-structured interview format is one that works particularly well with elite professionals (however defined) and those who are in protected positions of one sort or another, precisely because it provides a structure, which operates as a reminder about the purpose of the interview, reinforces the autonomous status of the researcher as some sort of expert, making it less likely that the interviewer will be sucked into the world of the person being researched (a potential danger of developing empathy). Since time is often a constraint in interviews of this sort, a semi-structured interview schedule also has the advantage of providing a framework that helps to ensure that all the important issues are covered in the time. Incidentally, if handled flexibly enough, it may also allow for more extended discussion if the developing interview relationship means that the discussion extends beyond the time initially agreed. (Despite their initial concerns about time, once they are allowed to talk about themselves and their priorities, even the most apparently time-constrained interviewees are often eager to continue.)

Within the same broad overall project, both approaches may be incorporated where they are able to complement each other – so, for example, in one project focused on rethinking everyday multiculture in new urban spaces and considering its relevance to policy, I have been involved with others in developing an approach that combines a more open-ended style that makes it possible for people to reflect on their own relationships with others, with one that involves semi-structured interviews with professionals and policy makers. The project also plans to utilize focus groups (Bennett 2002), and what have been called go-alongs – a form of interview in which the person being interviewed introduces the interviewer to their world (going along with them in a particular area of their daily life) (Kusenbach 2003).

For some urbanists recognizing the importance of the relationship between interviewer and interviewee in the research process is best understood as just one aspect of a wider rethinking of that process, in the context of community and place. They point to the possibility of participatory action research, in which emphasis is placed on identifying ways in which researchers can work together with others 'to examine a problematic situation or action to change it for the better', rather than one in which it is the task of the researcher to undertake research while others are (one way or another) identified as the subjects of research (Kindon et al. 2007b: 1; see also Pain and Kindon 2007).

Who is in control?

So far the emphasis of discussion has largely been on the extent to which the interview should be seen as a collaborative activity – a shared endeavour – through which knowledge is generated collectively, even if sometimes the expertise of the researcher does seem to trump the interpretation of the person being interviewed, however much it is couched in the language of co-production (Hollway and Jefferson 2000). But, like any interpersonal activity, interviews also incorporate power relations to which attention must be paid.

Historically the main concern has been that the researcher effectively shapes the agenda and in doing so shapes (and may even determine) the way in which the person being interviewed is able to respond. The fear is that in practice the researcher may take on the role of speaking for the interviewees, rather than allowing them to speak for themselves. As the ultimate author of any text, she or he – and you in the case of your dissertation – determines what is said, and there is always a danger that the person being interviewed may simply be mobilized as part of or inserted into a narrative developed by the researcher. This may be a particular problem when the research is focused on groups who are understood to be socially excluded or marginalized (for example, see Hopkins' discussion of the ethics involved in two projects, in one of which he was working with young Muslim men and in the other working with unaccompanied asylum-seeking children; Hopkins 2007).

In a sense, of course, the more open-ended and free narrative approaches that have been discussed already are intended to avoid these problems, even if the question remains of whether research subjects can just be enabled to speak or if there is a role for the researcher, if not speaking for them at least actively drawing out the implications (Kindon et al. 2007a). And, of course, the notion of empathy is an important aspect of this – in the sense that it repositions the interviewer as someone who needs to enter into the world of the interviewee, while not being absorbed into it.

But there is also an issue about the extent to which it is effectively the interviewee who is in control, as the researcher is captured in one way or another by the narrative performance of the person being interviewed. This is an issue whatever the form of interview (as expressed for example in the tension between observation and participation spelled out by Bondi) but can perhaps be most clearly illustrated from the example of interviews undertaken with people with a significantly higher status than the interviewer or in institutionally powerful positions, to the extent (for example) that the interviewer is dependent on her or his goodwill for the research to be undertaken. Linda McDowell (1992: 213) suggests that in some circumstances (for example when interviewing senior corporate or political actors) the interviewer may be positioned as supplicant, reliant on the goodwill of the interviewee rather than the dominant player. This may be an issue that you as a student need to reflect upon.

There is a danger in such a context that 'empathy' may translate into a process by which the researcher takes on the role of legitimating or supporting those who are the subject of the research. The 'inside dopester' (as Patrick Dunleavy [1980] so helpfully describes the role) becomes the person who knows his or her own elite better than anyone else and eagerly describes the inside stories of interaction, while losing any sense of broader directions of change (see also Cochrane 1998). In undertaking research on local authority finance professionals some years ago, the temptation for me to do this was almost unavoidable, as each treasurer being interviewed told me the same joke about the calculation of the main formula for the distribution of central government grant – there were only two people who understood it, the person talking to me and the person drawing up the formula in central government (who may, in any case, not have fully understood the implications) (Cochrane 1993).

This reinforces the need to maintain an appropriate distance in such interviews, and the semi-structured interview format can help with this, precisely because it adds a degree of formality and highlights the extent to which the researcher, too, has professional skills. But more important, perhaps, it is necessary to think explicitly about the ways in which power relations play across interviews in a range of contexts; Steve Pile (1991) helpfully reminds us that they may do so in a range of ways because the balance shifts through the research process, being negotiated by the participants without it always being made explicit. In other words, in principle, there may be nothing particularly special about elite interviews – what matters is that researchers think about the particular sets of relationships involved, before, during and after the interview (including the positionality of interviewer and interviewee; see England 1994).

The discussion so far has tended to view the interview as a one-off exercise – a joint performance or a set-piece encounter. The relationship can also be seen as a continuing one, to the extent that repeat interviews may be highly productive in two main ways. First, they make it possible to feed back conclusions or commentary (reopening the discussion), to clarify issues, to correct mistakes, as well as developing continuing dialogue. Second, they make it possible to involve the usual *subjects* of research in the development of the research. A repeat interview highlights the iterative aspect of the research process, learning and relearning as the process is pursued, but also in some cases providing support to those being interviewed as they develop policy or reflect on their own experiences.

The extent to which repeat interviews or feedback sessions can be sustained is in large part dependent on those who have been interviewed. They will already have given up their time to participate in the research, and taking up more time may not be particularly attractive to them. Or it may simply be too difficult to arrange a time for such an interview. My own experience has been mixed, particularly in the context of interviews conducted with senior officials in local government or universities. On occasion repeat visits have been welcomed, and this has generally been highly productive. In some cases feedback was organized with a wider group and this generated valuable feedback as conclusions were questioned, or further evidence brought to bear to help explain the ways in which particular decisions were made and approaches endorsed. The challenge for you is to build a relationship that makes it possible to return to those who have previously contributed to the development of the research and to make sure time is allowed for this, even while recognizing that it will not always be possible.

This is all part of an approach in which the aim is to maintain transparency and openness in the research process: those being interviewed have to be told what the research is about and how it will be used, as well as being told very clearly about guarantees of confidentiality, if appropriate. It is always salutary to remember that anyone who has agreed to be interviewed is doing you a favour, so that complaining about their reluctance to take part or noting their inability to deliver what is expected of them is inappropriate. All too often in their notes researchers are dismissive of those who are providing them with data. Academic researchers – such as those who lecture you at your university – are not investigative reporters seeking to expose the inconsistencies of those they are interviewing. On the contrary, part of the research process is to win over those who are assisting in the research and show them why it is worthwhile. Sometimes that means making it clear to people that they have something to contribute and will be listened to; sometimes it means making it clear to people that the process will contribute to policy development, allowing them to reflect more widely on the work in which they are involved.

The analysis of interviews generates its own challenges. The basic advice is clear enough: interviews should where possible be digitally recorded and transcribed.

That is not always possible, and where it is not, then it is important to take notes at the time and refresh them as soon as possible afterwards. Transcripts make it possible to analyse text using a range of software, which is developing all the time. The basic principles, however, do not rely on information technology because they are focused on forms of coding, which make it possible to extract themes. The coding will both flow from the questions that have been posed (the researcher's questions) but should also reflect what is said, which may drift away from the focus initially expected (and maybe even hoped for). Some people still prefer to do manual coding, because they feel it brings them closer to the text, but the important point is that you find a means of identifying key themes, and work with them across the various interviews. It is in this context that notes taken at the time of the interviews will also be helpful, in understanding the importance of what is now translated into rather cold text, whether on paper or computer screen. A conversation cannot simply be reduced to words on a page, however important they are. Such notes should identify how an interviewee is responding (maybe even facial expressions, and certainly any shifts in emphasis) but also, where appropriate, how the researcher responded to, or was involved in, the discussion – not just an empty sponge, absorbing what is being said.

The research diary that goes alongside the interviews is important for all these practical reasons, but it is also the place where a researcher is able actively and consistently to reflect on the actual research as it is being pursued. It sometimes feels as if the by-now universal injunction for researchers to be reflexive – to reflect on their own position within the research, on the prejudices and assumptions they bring, on their wider social positioning in terms of gender, ethnicity, class and age and so on – is little more than a form that has to be gone through or (possibly worse) an invitation to turn the focus on themselves and the difficulties they have faced. But in this context, it really is important to ensure that the interpersonal nature of the interview is recognized and its significance acknowledged. Sarah Neal and Sue Walters (2006) capture the peculiarity of the interview process very neatly in talking about being 'strangers asking strange questions'.

Despite hints at various points when actual projects were discussed, the focus of this chapter has been on interviewing itself and little more. It is important to recognize, however, that interviewing is unlikely to be the sole element of any urban research. Evidence drawn from content and discourse analysis, photography, ethnographies and questionnaires are all possible and familiar complements to interviews. Indeed a very strong and particular case would have to be made if interviews were to be used as a sole source of evidence. That, however, leaves us with the danger of simply stating that each research project draws on multiple methods, and that is indeed how some pieces of research are justified. But that is not enough. If it is important to be clear where methods are complementary, it is equally necessary to understand where they are not; there is an easy temptation to promise a multi-method approach only to discover that what is being brought together is not really compatible.

Conclusion

By now, the picture of what initially seemed like such a simple activity – talking to people about what they do or know – has, I hope, been suitably disrupted, but equally, I hope that the value of interviews in a range of research contexts remains clear. Above all, it is important to start by thinking in each case what the interviews are for and so what style of interview (from open-ended free narrative to semi-structured) would be most appropriate in that context. All interviews are performances, but both interviewer and interviewee are playing parts in the performance, which makes it important for researchers to reflect on the changing balance between participants throughout the interview. The attempt to balance observation and empathetic participation are central to any effective interview. A degree of modesty is required from any researcher because the interview process is a shared endeavour and those taking part deserve to be respected. If possible, repeat interviews or feedback sessions with those who have been interviewed are helpful, and openness with them about the research and its conduct is essential. And finally, it is important to recognize that interviewing is in most cases only going to be one of several methods used in any piece of research fieldwork – but what matters is to be clear what each of the methods being used contributes to answering the questions around which the research is focused.

Frequently Asked Questions

1. What are interviews for?

There is a danger of taking interviews for granted as an unproblematic source of evidence in researching the city, so it is important to think carefully about what they can be expected to deliver in answering particular research questions. Although they can be used to generate information (in a sense using those being interviewed as sources – as informal researchers), they are most valuable as means of allowing and enabling people to discuss their own experience, their own position, and encouraging them to reflect on their understanding of it. Interviews are normally used within a wider menu of research methods complementing each other as part of an integrated research strategy.

2. What is an interview?

An interview has to be understood both as a performance (in which both researcher and researched are involved) and as a collaborative

(Continued)

(Continued)

process, a relationship that may go beyond the particular moment of the interview itself. Each interview involves a process of negotiation between the participants. The implications of this are significant, because it implies a continuing process of reflection by the person undertaking the interview, the building of an empathetic relationship with the person being interviewed, but also a self-conscious distancing based on the recognition of the purpose of the interview – clarity about what is expected from it. In that sense (as Bondi puts it) the interviewer must be an observer as well as a participant. Different sorts of interviews – from open-ended to semi-structured – will be appropriate in different contexts, depending on the focus of the research.

3. Who is in control?

Once one accepts that interviews have to be understood in the terms discussed above, then it is important to reflect on the power relations that may be expressed in practices of interviewing. One fear is that the interviewer may effectively shape the process in ways that leave the people being interviewed as subordinate in one way or another – dependent on the researcher to define which responses are legitimate and which can be discounted. In other words there is a risk that the power relations involved may limit rather than enable other voices to be heard. A parallel worry relates to interviews with members of political or business elites, who may come to determine the research agenda because the researcher is dependent on their goodwill. It is important to bear these concerns in mind, and to develop strategies that reduce the risk of either failing to allow the researched to speak for themselves or positioning the researcher (however unwittingly) as mouthpiece for the powerful.

Follow Up References

Bondi, L. (2003) Empathy and identification: conceptual resources for feminist field-work. *ACME: An International E-Journal for Critical Geographers*, 2: 64–76.

This article highlights the importance of taking empathy seriously in the interview process, as well as exploring the continued need to remain distanced in key respects – to be able to observe as well as participate

Hollway, W. and Jefferson, T. (2000) *Doing Qualitative Research Differently: Free Association, Narrative and the Interview Method.* London: Sage.

The case for using an open-ended approach to interviewing, drawing on psycho-therapeutic understandings, is developed in this book, which also presents case studies of research in practice. While this approach may not be appropriate in all research situations, the case is set out systematically and clearly here.

Kindon, S., Pain, R. and Kesby, M. (eds) (2007) *Participatory Action Research Methods and Approaches: Connecting People, Participation and Place.* Abingdon: Routledge.

This collection delivers a series of interesting case studies of participatory action research in a range of contexts, and shows how interviews can be incorporated into the process. It explores some of the possible implications of understanding (place-based) research as a collaborative endeavour.

Savage, M. (2010) *Identities and Social Change in Britain since 1940: The Politics of Method.* Oxford: Oxford University Press.

This is a fascinating book which combines a consideration of social change in Britain with a review of the methods adopted by social scientists in trying to make sense of it (and in some ways to define it). Chapter 7, in particular, reflects on the rise of the interview as a method in the post-1945 period.

Smith, K. (2006) Problematising power relations in elite interviews. *Geoforum*, 37: 643–53.

The question of how best to understand the ways in which power relations operate in elite interviews is a recurrent one, and this paper begins to question some of the dominant ways in which they have been conceptualized in the past, offering different ways of thinking about them.

References

Allen, J. (2003) *Lost Geographies of Power.* Oxford: Blackwell.
Bennett, K. (2002) Interviews and focus groups, in P. Shurmer-Smith (ed.), *Doing Cultural Geography.* London: Sage, pp. 151–62.
Bondi, L. (2003) Empathy and identification: conceptual resources for feminist fieldwork. *ACME, An International E-Journal for Critical Geographies*, 2: 64–76.
Bondi, L. (2005) Making connections and thinking through emotions: between geography and psychotherapy. *Transactions of the Institute of British Geographers*, NS 30: 433–48.
Cloke, P., Cook, I., Crang, P., Goodwin, M., Painter, J. and Philo, C. (2004) *Practising Human Geography.* London: Sage.

Cochrane, A. (1993) From financial control to strategic management: the changing faces of accountability in British local government. *Accounting, Auditing and Accountability Journal*, 6: 31–52.

Cochrane, A. (1998) Illusions of power: interviewing local elites. *Environment and Planning A*, 30: 2121–32.

Dunleavy, P. (1980) *Urban Political Analysis: The Politics of Collective Consumption*. London: Macmillan.

England, K. (1994) Getting personal: reflexivity, positionality and feminist research. *The Professional Geographer*, 46: 80–9.

Gubrium, J. and Holstein, J. (2002) From the individual interview to the interview society, in J. Gubrium and J. Holstein (eds), *Handbook of Interview Research: Context and Method*. London: Sage, pp. 3–32.

Hammersley, M. (2008) *Questioning Qualitative Inquiry: Critical Essays*. London: Sage.

Hollway, W. and Jefferson, T. (2000) *Doing Qualitative Research Differently: Free Association, Narrative and the Interview Method*. London: Sage.

Hopkins, P. (2007) Positionalities and knowledge: negotiating ethics in practice. *ACME: An International E-Journal for Critical Geographies*, 6: 386–94.

Judge, D., Stoker, G. and Wolman, H. (eds) (1995) *Theories of Urban Politics*. London: Sage.

Kindon, S., Pain, R. and Kesby, M. (2007a) Introduction: connecting people, participation and place, in S. Kindon, R. Pain and M. Kesby (eds), *Participatory Action Research Methods and Approaches: Connecting People, Participation and Place*. Abingdon: Routledge, pp. 1–18.

Kindon, S., Pain, R. and Kesby, M. (eds) (2007b) *Participatory Action Research Methods and Approaches: Connecting People, Participation and Place*. Abingdon: Routledge.

Kusenbach, M. (2003) Street phenomenology: the go-along as ethnographic research tool. *Ethnography*, 43: 445–8.

Latour, B. (1996) *Aramis, or the Love of Technology*. Cambridge, MA: Harvard University Press.

McDowell, L. (1992) Valid games? A response to Erica Schoenberger. *The Professional Geographer*, 44: 212–15.

Neal, S. and McLaughlin, E. (2009) Researching up? Interviews, emotionality and policy making elites. *Journal of Social Policy*, 38: 689–707.

Neal, S. and Walters, S. (2006) Strangers asking strange questions? A methodological narrative on researching belonging and identity in the English countryside. *Journal of Rural Studies*, 22: 279–97.

Pain, R. and Kindon, S. (2007) Participatory geographies. *Environment and Planning A*, 39: 2807–12.

Peck, J. and Theodore, N. (2012) Following the policy: a distended case study approach. *Environment and Planning A*, 44: 21–30.

Pile, S. (1991) Practising interpretative geography. *Transactions of the Institute of British Geographers*, NS 16: 405–21.

Raco, M. (1999) Researching the new urban governance: an examination of closure, access and complexities of institutional research. *Area*, 31: 271–9.

Savage, M. (2010) *Identities and Social Change in Britain since 1940: The Politics of Method.* Oxford: Oxford University Press.

Silverman, D. (2004) *Qualitative Research: Theory, Method and Practice* (2nd edn). London: Sage.

Smith, K. (2006) Problematising power relations in 'elite' interviews. *Geoforum,* 37: 643–53.

Ward, K. and Jones, M. (1999) Researching local elites: reflexivity, 'situatedness' and political-temporal contingency. *Geoforum,* 30: 301–12.

5

URBAN ETHNOGRAPHIC RESEARCH

Kate Swanson

Introduction

Scholars have called upon geographers to employ ethnographic research methods for some time; despite this, ethnography has remained largely on the margins of the discipline. This is finally beginning to change. Urban geographers, in particular, are increasingly using ethnographic methods to investigate numerous social issues, including homelessness, gentrification, policing, migration, street vendors, activism, poverty and youth sub-cultures, among others. In a rapidly globalizing world, with exacerbated inequalities between the rich and poor, ethnography is ideally suited for unravelling the politics of survival at the micro-scale as situated within larger socio-economic processes.

In this chapter I discuss some of the main issues surrounding *doing* ethnography. Based upon my own experiences conducting extensive and in-depth research with young street vendors and beggars in Ecuador's largest cities (see Swanson 2010), I discuss some of the strengths and limitations of ethnography. In doing so, I hope to provide guidance for those of you embarking upon the exciting, yet often daunting, task of undertaking your own dissertation research. I frame this chapter around the theme of urban poverty and marginality, a pressing topic in so many cities around the world, particularly where gaps between the rich and poor continue to rise. Before delving into specifics regarding how to do ethnography, however, I briefly discuss how geographers have approached ethnographic research. I suggest that the way geographers *do* ethnography is not entirely consistent with traditional methods employed by anthropologists and sociologists.

Ethnographic research in geography

Ethnography often involves unequal power dynamics between the researcher and the researched. For instance, while some may focus on homeless youth in Hollywood (Ruddick 1996), others may focus on investment bankers in London (McDowell 1997), both of which reflect situations where there are obvious power imbalances. Beginning in the late 1960s, scholars began to explore these unequal power dynamics more critically, particularly in the discipline of anthropology. This shift was especially spurred on by the 1967 publication of revered ethnographer Bronislaw Malinowski's personal fieldwork diaries. Malinowski was a scholar who spent years researching culture, magic and exchange systems among the Trobriand Islanders in the South Pacific. Since the publication of his first book in 1922, his vigorous research methods became the model for ethnographic fieldwork, particularly in terms of participant observation. During his research he realized that actions do not always match intent, meaning people often say one thing, but do another entirely. He argued that by living with a group, spending time with them and integrating oneself into their culture, researchers become better able to experience culture as an 'insider', thus gaining greater insight. This was a significant shift from the so-called armchair anthropologists of before who had long theorized about cultures from afar, in keeping with colonial and imperial traditions. Yet, when Malinowski's private thoughts were published after his death, his diaries revealed him to be a 'crabbed, self-preoccupied, hypochondriacal narcissist, whose fellow-feeling for the people he lived with was limited in the extreme' (Geertz 1967: 12). His diaries demonstrated quite clearly that the way he chose to represent himself in his scholarly texts was altogether different than reality. Hence began the crisis of representation.

Scholars came to realize that writing about culture involved representations that were necessarily partial, partisan and problematic (Goodall 2000). They realized that rather than providing unbiased depictions of cultures, ethnographers cannot help but provide incomplete and subjective representations. Clifford (1986) went so far as to call ethnographies 'partial truths', or even fictions, due to inevitable omissions and the silencing of certain voices. These scholars also recognized that ethnographic writing is profoundly shaped by the ethnographer's positionality, or by their individual social locations and life experiences. For instance, Malinowski's research would have produced very different results had it been conducted by a native Trobriand Islander as opposed to a young Polish interloper. Thereafter, scholars tried to distance themselves from the presumed objective, ethnographic gaze to write more self-reflexive and openly subjective ethnographies. Or, as stated by Goodall

(2000: 78), scholars 'began turning our gaze away from those whom we were studying to the process we used to study and write, and within that turning, we came full circle, back to ourselves'.

This self-reflexive turn had a particularly strong impact on feminist geography. In a 1994 special issue of *Professional Geographer*, scholars Cindi Katz, Kim England, Heidi Nast, Audrey Kobayashi and Melissa Gilbert wrote influential papers concerning the ethics and power dynamics involved in field research. They encouraged researchers to recognize and problematize the cultural baggage, biases and uneven balances of power that are inherent in research. They pushed researchers to collaborate with and learn from their participants, a fundamentally different approach than in the past. These scholars also raised key questions concerning the ethical outcomes of research and our responsibilities to those with whom we work. These types of concerns have had profound impacts upon academic disciplines today, particularly as evidenced through university ethics committees and institutional review boards that are tasked to review student and faculty research proposals.

Recognizing the uneven power balances in research pushed scholars to question some of the larger structural factors shaping these personal and political inequalities, particularly in cities. While sociologists have been concerned with urban inequality since at least the turn of the twentieth century (Park and Burgess 1925), increasing concentrations of poverty and marginality at the end of the twentieth century reinvigorated academic debates on the issue. Critical urban scholars, including Loïc Wacquant (2004), Philippe Bourgois (2003), Katherine Newman (1999), Mitchell Duneier (1999) and Michael Burawoy and his graduate students (2001), published powerful, moving and deeply reflexive ethnographies, which had a tremendous impact on the ways in which urban poverty and marginality are perceived. For instance, Newman, who writes to dispel myths surrounding the working poor in Harlem, New York, begins her book with a poignant and sobering account of the struggles of young Jamal and Kathy as they try to make ends meet on Jamal's meagre Burger Barn salary. Her work explores the social and structural conditions that make it so difficult for poor families to get ahead in the United States of America. Loïc Wacquant, a French sociologist, spent three years training at a boxing gym in a Chicago 'ghetto' in order to understand the exploitation and social ostracization of African Americans. In an emotionally intense ethnography, Philippe Bourgois describes how he spent four years living in East Harlem, and hanging out in a crackhouse, in order to explore poverty and ethnic segregation in one of the most expensive cities in the world. His account is, at times, brutal because he believes that '[t]he depth and overwhelming pain and terror of the experience of poverty and racism in the United States needs to be talked about openly and confronted squarely, even if that makes us uncomfortable' (Bourgois 2003: 18).

Geographers have been slower to engage in urban ethnography, despite calls to the contrary (Jackson, 1985: Herbert, 2000), as indicated at the beginning of this chapter. This could be because geographers approach ethnography in ways that are different than anthropologists and sociologists, to the extent that many are reluctant to label their work 'ethnographic', strictly speaking. For instance, geographers tend to use mixed methods (for example, combining participant observation and interviews with geospatial techniques), conduct fieldwork over several short but intensive periods of time (as opposed to living in the field for up to three years), and often publish their work in peer-reviewed journal articles rather than in books. In fact, a few have proposed relabelling the ethnographic work that geographers do as *geo-ethnography* (see Anderson 2012; Matthews et al. 2005; Till 2005), since our methods do not always sit easily within tradition- ally defined norms of ethnography. Although limited in number, geographers have produced a range of fascinating and important ethnographies in cities, including work on urban policing in Los Angeles (Herbert 1997), global migrants in London (Wills et al. 2010), slum settlements in Delhi (Datta 2011), street-vendor struggles in Mexico City (Crossa 2009), human rights activism in Buenos Aires (Bosco 2006), world-class city making in Delhi (Ghertner 2011), prisons and race in Los Angeles (Gilmore 2007), street kids in New York City (Gibson 2011), and Indian diasporas and urban development in Kolkata (Bose 2007), to name a few. What makes these ethnographies geographic is that they cut across scales to explore complex local–global interconnections. For instance, in discussing transnational migrants in the city of London, May et al. (2007: 161) state that 'instead of holding apart the "global" and the "local", we need to embrace a relational view of scale: examining the variety of scales at which processes shaping global city labour markets unfold, and the manner in which processes operating at one scale help constitute processes operating at another.'

There is also a growing group of emerging scholars who are using urban ethnography – or perhaps geo-ethnography – to produce important new scholar- ship. Some of these research topics include panhandlers in Vancouver (Proudfoot 2011), social reproduction of everyday life in Manhattan (Anderson 2012), gentri- fication and resistance in Rio de Janeiro (Goode et al. 2013), politics of urban redevelopment and displacement in Mumbai (Doshi 2011), day labourers in San Diego (Crotty and Bosco 2008), homelessness and citizenship in Washington State (Sparks 2011), and architectural nation-building in Astana, Kazakhstan (Koch 2010). Using geographic tools and techniques, geographers are reshaping ethnog- raphy in ways that may allow for more nuanced understandings of how social and spatial relations are expressed across scales in an increasingly complex world.

Preparing for research

Given this background to ethnography, the question remains: how do we prepare for and *do* ethnography? As noted by DeLyser and Starrs (2001), knowing how to con- duct field research is not an innate skill. Yet, teaching ethnography is tricky since so many lessons learned no longer apply once we enter the field. The following advice was offered to graduate students by Bernard Nietschmann (2001: 177), a renowned geography professor at the University of California, Berkeley, from 1977 to 2000:

1. Prior to leaving for the field, carefully draw up a plot plan, list of materials, etc.
2. Immediately upon arriving at the field, throw away item No. 1 above. Now that you've seen the field, it obviously won't work anyway.

Now, don't throw away your proposals just yet! Clearly, having a carefully planned proposal, with core research questions, will help guide your research throughout the length of your fieldwork. But it is important to recognize that some of your questions and plans may change once you actually begin your fieldwork. When I began my doctoral fieldwork in Quito, Ecuador, I arrived with the intention of staying for nine months, but I ended up staying for eighteen. My research proposal detailed a rigorous plan to work with migrant street-working children, and outlined a series of people and organizations to liaise with when I arrived. Of course, once I saw the field, my research plans changed. The core substance of my research remained the same; what differed were the specifics. While my research proposal was broadly titled 'Globalization and Childhood: A Case Study of Street and Working Children in Quito, Ecuador', my final dissertation was more about urban restructuring and exclusion; gender and public space; migrant youth identities and childhood; racialization of indigenous peoples; and begging and informal sector strategies. Globalization and childhood were themes that ran through my work, but I discovered new themes as well. This is why *doing* ethnography is important. Theorizing about the nature of urban poverty from the classroom, for instance, is an altogether different experience than going out into the community, talking to people about their experiences, participating in community events, and experiencing first hand how inequality takes shape on the ground. Through these ethnographic experiences, researchers often realize that the questions they were asking at the beginning of their projects were the wrong questions. This is an important step in undertaking solid, ethnographic research.

Another caveat for doing ethnography is that you must be willing to spend a significant amount of time with the people and society you are studying. While I spent eighteen months in the field, few undergraduate or master's students will have this luxury of time. For this reason, ethnography may not be an appropriate method for everyone. For instance, a one-week class field trip to Mallorca is an insufficient amount of time to build an ethnographic project. However, ethnography may be appropriate if you have already built trust within a particular community at home. For instance, perhaps you are a roller derby fanatic and have been involved in this sub-culture for years. For your dissertation, you would like to study girl culture, power and politics as they take shape in London's roller derby world. In this case, you may already have gatekeepers, key contacts and an established reputation within your chosen community, thus garnering you a significant level of trust. Ethnography may be an appropriate research method in this type of scenario.

Doing research

The time has come to begin your fieldwork, but where and how do you begin? If you are at all like me, you may find starting projects difficult. When I began my doctoral fieldwork, I had never been to Ecuador before. I had previously travelled around South America, including to a number of Andean countries, but Ecuador was new to me. This was because I had switched my research focus from child waste pickers in Vietnam to street working children in Ecuador during the second year of my PhD programme (which was a fairly substantial change of focus!). This meant that I had a steep learning curve upon arrival in Ecuador. Perhaps for this reason, I became very tentative. Time began to pass by quickly and I had little to show in return. While I had convinced myself that I was becoming acclimatized to Ecuadorian culture, becoming better at Spanish, and that I was engaging in extensive participant observation (all true), my time in Ecuador was limited, and my advisers were beginning to wonder what was going on. I received pleading messages from my advisers such as, 'Kate, I am concerned about you. I see you are working very hard at different things but you are not being strategic about developing logical connections in your research plan.' This was true. I was dabbling in many areas but was not being strategic. In fact, I was somewhat overwhelmed and unsure where to begin. Part of my hesitation stemmed from a fear that no one would want to talk to me, or that I would take up too much of people's time, or possibly worse, that I would ask bad questions. I figured that the more time I spent absorbing local culture and reading secondary literature sources, the more prepared I would become. However, research projects run on a timeline, so this was clearly not a viable long-term strategy. (Note: this is an especially important point for undergraduate and master's students, who have less time in which to produce their dissertations!) Eventually, I mustered up the nerve to pick up the phone and begin calling my list of potential key informants. For me, that first phone call and subsequent appointment were a crucial step, as I knew this meant that I was committed: I *would* be interviewing someone important within the next week, and there was no turning back. Of course, sometimes I did get rejected, sometimes I did take up too much of people's time, and I sometimes definitely did ask bad questions. In fact, the first interview I did was with a representative from CONAIE, Ecuador's leading indigenous political organization, and it ended with him giving me a brochure about the organization and telling me to go home and study it! But the more interviews I did, the more skilled I became at asking questions and navigating the social dynamics involved in an interview (see Chapter 4, this volume). My greatest surprise during this process was that I learned that people liked talking to me and, in fact, many loved telling me all about themselves and their views on the world. If you think about it, people rarely have opportunities to talk exclusively about themselves and their thoughts, and I found that many really relished this opportunity. The more questions I asked, the more they warmed up and the conversation flowed. Once I discovered this, I became much more confident and my research progressed rapidly. But – before you can get to this point, you have to make that first phone call, or send that first email, or introduce yourself to that intimidating-looking person at the community meeting. You will make blunders to begin with, but this is normal; like anything, the more you practise, the better you get.

Making appointments with officials was one thing, but approaching random working children on the streets was another. My first few attempts to approach children were interesting, but it was clear that these children had no reason to trust me. For this reason, I needed a good gatekeeper or someone who could provide me with entrance into this community. Finding a good gatekeeper is critical, as this person can make or break your research. The gatekeeper you choose must be someone who is trusted, who has a strong social network, and who is willing to introduce you to those you wish to work with. For instance, say you are interested in researching gang culture and violence. Due to strict hierarchies within this sub-culture, it matters a lot who you choose as your gatekeeper. Do you choose someone from a non-governmental organization, who actively works to get young people out of gangs? If you choose this route, the young people you meet with will likely be those who are trying to leave or have already left the gang, and may paint a very negative portrait of their experiences. This will represent a particular truth. What if you have access to someone in a gang? This would provide a very different portrait of gang life, although it could put you at a greater risk of actually experiencing violence. Dennis Rodgers (2007: 455), an anthropologist conducting research on poverty and violence in Managua, Nicaragua, describes how he managed to befriend one of his community's more prominent gang members, and eventually became initiated into the gang through three rites involving varying degrees of violence and criminality. In doing so, however, he gained an entirely different understanding of gang life. He states, 'becoming a member of the gang and adopting certain behaviour patterns allowed me to understand much more viscerally particular aspects of gang life. I might well never have understood the nature of the love that the *pandilleros* [gang members] felt for their neighbourhood, for example, because it was something that lay outside my intellectual horizons.' The point here is not to encourage you to go out and join a gang in the name of research; rather, it is to consider how different types of gatekeepers fundamentally shape the outcomes of research. Your gatekeeper's positionality and biases will affect the ways in which you are perceived, and how people respond to your research questions. Only after you have spent significant time with a community will people begin to trust you for your own merits.

In my case, I spent three months working with one organization before I realized that they would not be able to provide me with access to the children I was interested in. I wanted to learn more about the young indigenous children who begged and sold *chicles* – or chewing gum – in the city's main tourist districts. By asking a lot of questions, I eventually found a woman who was directing a programme for indigenous street vendors and beggars in Quito. She and her small organization were the only ones working with this group of youth and I was lucky to have found her. Janeth had many years of experience working at a shelter for indigenous migrants in Quito, and she was also directing a few development projects in a group of rural communities where most of these indigenous migrants were from. After we met and I told her about my research interests, she invited me to work with her both in the rural communities and on the streets of Quito. Since she was under-funded, she needed help. Due to her years of experience working with migrants, Janeth was able to provide access in crucial ways. In fact, I do not think I could have completed my project without her. The only difficulty was that Janeth's politics were explicitly anti-begging, as she was trying to provide young people with alternative means of earning income. However, I was trying to present myself as neutral and non-judgemental. Because of my connection to Janeth, most community members assumed that my politics were the same as hers, meaning that few would talk to me about their involvement in begging – at least, to begin with. It was a long time before people trusted me enough to open up.

Once you have secured your gatekeeper and have been invited into a community, you must learn how to observe. This is easier said than done. In our society, we often busy ourselves when we are alone, and rarely let our eyes and minds roam. For instance, when you are alone, how often do you simply sit and watch life go by? How long do you leave your phone in your pocket without checking it for texts, news or connecting with friends? Alternatively, perhaps you prefer to bury your head in a book, rather than sit awkwardly by yourself. Some people are better at being alone with their thoughts than others, but for many people this is a difficult task. In order to practise observing, I urge you to begin detaching your eyes from your gadgets when you are out and about and begin watching the world around you with fresh eyes. In doing so, you may begin to look at things differently and notice other things that you have never paid attention to before.

Ethnography involves participant observation, which is a practice that recog-nizes that what people say is often inconsistent with what they do. For instance, in my research young people often told me that they never begged, yet I would later see them begging on street corners. Participant observation means learning how to participate within a community, but also being able to step back and ana-lyse events as they occur. Some people choose to fully immerse themselves in a particular culture or community, whereas others prefer a role more on the side-lines. By participating in a community researchers are often able to understand the social dynamics, power relations, perceptions, struggles and experiences of the group at a depth that they may not have been able to otherwise. For myself, my role as a participant increased as community members became more comfortable with me and as I became more comfortable with them. My weeks involved both visiting the rural communities and accompanying Janeth during her street out-reach work in Quito. During this process I learned that the vast majority of indigenous women and children begging and selling *chicles* in Quito were from one small community in particular, named Calhuasí. Men and older boys also migrated from this community to work as shoe shiners, and sometimes to sell goods on buses. By spending a large amount of time in their village, I was able to gain significant trust, which was crucial to my success on the streets. I eventually reached a stage where a family agreed to host me in their home in Calhuasí for a period of one month. This was groundbreaking as it allowed me to become more fully integrated into the community, to the extent that I was even asked to be a *comadre* (which literally means 'co-mother', but in practice is more similar to the role of a godmother) to a young child. Thereafter, when Calhuaseños saw me (and my dog, as I moved to the community with my dog), on the streets, they immediately recognized me as a familiar and friendly face. Young people, my dog and I would often 'hang out' in a city park, playing Frisbee or talking about their experiences on the streets. Sometimes they would use my recorder to sing songs and giggle while they played back their performances. Eventually, many young people started coming to my apartment to visit, as I lived close to a corner where many worked. During this time, we would chat, eat and look at pictures of their families and friends on my laptop. These became great impromptu interview situations, as many were eager to tell me all about their lives.

An important issue during any ethnographic project is the matter of informed consent. This is particularly important when working with young people and marginalized groups. Prior to interviewing people, whether formally or informally, you must be explicit concerning what your research project is about, the expected outcomes, and any possible risks (or benefits) to participants. Your participants must voluntarily choose to be part of your project and must be deemed capable of making this informed decision. If you are working with minors, for instance, you might need to seek the consent of their parents or guardians, or be able to prove that they are emancipated minors (in the case of some street children, for instance). Unequal power dynamics are another issue that can shape research in unexpected ways. Many research projects on poverty necessarily focus on marginalized groups. Yet, those who direct these research projects are often from more privileged middle-income and upper-income backgrounds. Race, ethnicity, gender, sexuality, age, ability and other identity markers can also critically inform positions of power within research projects. For instance, in my work the unequal power dynamics were difficult to ignore; I was a privileged, white Westerner, able to jet around the world to study impoverished, racialized, indigenous beggars in Ecuador. At the micro scale my power was sometimes subverted in unexpected ways, for instance when I was treated like a child owing to my presumed incompetence regarding household maintenance. In one instance, the parents of my Calhuaseño host family left for three days but chose to put their 12-year-old daughter in charge instead of me. On another occasion, an 8-year-old boy was directed to cook my lunch in his mother's absence (see Swanson 2008). Nevertheless, the reality was that in the grand scheme of things, my positionality allowed me great privilege and access to spaces and information that others may not have been able to attain. Being aware of these power dynamics is crucial in order to conduct ethical research, and help you anticipate how your positionality might affect your research plans. Most universities have ethics committees or institutional review boards that can provide detailed guidance on how to obtain informed consent, and sometimes how to navigate unequal power relations.

Writing up research

During your research it is vital that your take extensive field notes every single day you are in the field. If you do not write things down, you will forget them. Allow me to repeat that: you *will* forget things. Write *everything* down. I would further advise you to type up your notes at the end of every day and flush them out with further details. I worked in Ecuador with an anthropologist who was very disciplined about her field notes and would spend at least two hours a night typing them up when they were still fresh in her mind, regardless of what else was happening in her life. She made this task her priority. This saved her hours and hours of tedious work typing up and making sense of her notes later, as I had to do. Being disciplined about this is important because your field notes will become the raw data of your project. As noted by Goodall, 'fieldnotes are less about what you initially "see" and "experience" than they are about *connecting* those fieldwork details to larger and more self-reflexive issues. Which is to say that what fieldnotes represent is one part recorded observations and experiences and two parts interpretation, or how you learn to *hear in* and *through* all of that' (2000: 86, original emphasis). In other words, your field notes represent your first step towards making sense of the cultural world you are studying.

The next step is to weave this into a richly written account. Many ethnographers rely heavily upon first-person quotes, which help stories come to life through the words of their informants. These quotes add character, tone, and richness. Others use impressionistic styles and write in a way that demands attention. For instance, Danny Hoffman (2008: 123) begins his urban ethnography regarding the life of a young man in Freetown, Sierra Leone as follows:

> Mohammed breaks rocks. It is 'work' only in that it fills his days and demands much of his slender body. Smashing stone into gravel with a small hammer is one of the tasks Mohammed performs for the right to remain a squatter, a caretaker of someone else's land. What money Mohammed has comes in other unreliable and hard-won ways: hustling on the streets of Freetown; performing odd jobs for mechanics or welders; or, his most lucrative activity these days, running *djamba* [marijuana] to the Liberian border.

Hoffman draws the reader in with his prose, but also hints at the rich themes at the centre of his ethnography. He continues in a self-reflexive manner by bringing himself into the story and describing his relationship to Mohammed. This comes back to your positionality: in writing your ethnography you must understand how your identity shapes your research results and the interpretation of these results. For many, this is difficult work. As noted by Heynen (2006: 928), 'most of us have been trained to write in the third person, to be objective, to be uncritical and apolitical, to not put more of ourselves in our work. We have been trained to keep the pain and suffering of the world at arm's length.' This is not the case with ethnography; instead we are encouraged to put more of ourselves into our work, be subjective, be explicit about how our positionality shapes our representations, and to put our personal politics up front.

Conclusion

Many of us hope that our research results will be significant enough to matter, or to somehow make a difference in the world. For those concerned with social justice, poverty and marginality, ethnography is a particularly potent methodology. By spending time with people and experiencing their day-to-day realities, ethnographic research has rich potential to unravel myths and challenge assumptions and stereotypes. However, ethnography is not without limits. As Gowan (2010: 19) notes, 'the awkward intimacies of ethnographic method have a tendency to bring up excruciating dilemmas, pressing us to wrestle particularly intensely with questions of representation, reciprocity, accountability and other "power effects".' These awkward intimacies and dilemmas can last long term, as ethnographers often become very close to their research participants. For instance, I conducted my research in Ecuador ten years ago yet I am still in regular contact with those I worked with, some of whom have now migrated to New York City. Research relationships generally do not end when the funding runs out, and ethnographers must be prepared to make long-term personal and emotional commitments. For some, this is a strength, whereas for others, it is a weakness. Another critique of ethnography is that research results can sometimes be interpreted in unintended ways, particularly for research focused on marginalized groups. Philippe Bourgois (2003: 18) quotes Laura Nader, who states, 'Don't study the poor and the powerless because everything you say about them will be used against them.' Ethnographers must be very sensitive to the political implications of writing about the lives of the poor and marginalized, lest their results be misinterpreted. Regardless of whether you are 'studying up' or 'studying down', it is crucial to think through the ethical implications of your findings. What broader impacts will your research have? How will your results be used? In sum, ethnography is a powerful methodological tool and one that is under-utilized in geography. By using our social-spatial training, geographers are well situated to produce engaging and innovative geo-ethnographies to reshape discourses of poverty and marginality in cities around the world.

Frequently Asked Questions

1. What are the advantages of ethnography?

Ethnographic methods allow researchers to produce in-depth accounts of particular issues in ways that more quantitative research cannot. Using ethnography, researchers can capture individual voices and stories to create richly written narratives, weaving theory and empirics together.

2. What are the disadvantages of ethnography?

Ethnography rarely produces statistically significant results, as it aims for depth rather than breadth of data. Some argue that because of this, little conclusive scientific evidence can be gleaned from ethnographic data. However, ethnography is not designed to produce this sort of knowledge; rather, it is ideally suited for in-depth case studies that can inform broader theory.

3. Should I use ethnography in my research project?

Ethnography is appropriate when you intend to spend a sustained amount of time with a particular group of people, sub-culture or society. Ethnography requires trust and this can rarely be obtained over a period of two or three weeks. Rather, you must be willing to invest time and energy in order to build up long-term relationships, which will result in better access and insight.

4. When is ethnography inappropriate?

Ethnography is inappropriate when you have a limited amount of time, such as during short class field trips. It may be appropriate to use ethnographic methods during these field trips (such as participant observation, interviews, diaries, field notes, photos, etc.) but you will not be in the field long enough to have conducted an 'ethnography'. Ethnography is also inappropriate if you cannot gain the confidence of the community, sub-culture or society you are interested in. Some communities are mistrustful of outsiders, particularly researchers, and it may be very difficult for you to gain entrance. Will your research be useful to this community? How will you be invited into this community? What skill or ability can you

(Continued)

(Continued)

offer in exchange? Reciprocity is crucial in ethnographic research, particularly in terms of building strong relationships. If you cannot gain a community's trust, you may need to find a different research method, or perhaps a different research topic.

5. What field research techniques do ethnographers use?

Ethnographers use a range of techniques. Participant observation is a key technique, along with qualitative interviews and secondary data collection. Other techniques vary but can include photography, mapping, diaries, notes, videos, questionnaires, focus groups, surveys, and participatory action research, among others. They key to ethnography is to spend a sustained amount of time with people in order to immerse yourself within a particular society or culture.

Follow Up References

Bourgois, P. (2003) *In Search of Respect: Selling Crack in El Barrio,* 2nd edn. Cambridge, MA: Cambridge University Press.

This book is an excellent example of a powerful urban ethnography. Based upon four years of research in a Harlem ghetto during the 1990s crack epidemic, Bourgois has written a moving and disturbing book that explores deep racial, gendered and socio-structural inequalities in American society.

Goodall, H.L., Jr (2000) *Writing the New Ethnography.* New York: Altamira Press.

This is a fun, well-written book that outlines the process of doing and writing up ethnographic research. At the end of every chapter there are a series of helpful writing exercises on various topics, including framing a research question, developing a voice, and ethics in research and writing, among others.

Herbert, S. (2000) For ethnography. *Progress in Human Geography,* 24: 550–68.

Herbert challenges a number of common criticisms of ethnography in this paper, including: 'that it is unscientific; that it is too limited to enable generalization; and that it fails to consider its inherent representational practices'. After countering each of these claims, he concludes by encouraging geographers to engage in more and more rigorous ethnography.

Swanson, K. (2008) Witches, children and Kiva-the-research-dog: striking problems encountered in the field. *Area,* 40: 55–64.

This is a methods paper wherein I discuss some of the problems and issues that I encountered during my ethnographic fieldwork in Ecuador, particularly concerning power, privilege, and vulnerability. I also reflect upon a particularly unorthodox research method: using my dog as a research assistant.

Watson, A. and Till, K. (2010) Ethnography and participant observation, in D. DeLyser, S. Herber, S. Aitken, M. Crang and L. McDowell (eds), *The Sage Handbook of Qualitative Geography.* Thousand Oaks, CA: Sage, pp. 121–37.

Watson and Till review the literature on geography and ethnography in this chapter, while also discussing how they have used ethnography in their own research and writing. For those interested in qualitative research in geography more generally, this Sage Handbook is highly valuable and provides helpful guidance and thoughts on autoethnography, interviewing, archival research, and discourse analysis, among other topics.

References

Anderson, C. (2012) Lost in space? Ethnography and the disparate geographies of social process. *Professional Geographer,* 64: 276–85.

Bosco, F. (2006) The Madres de Plaza de Mayo and three decades of human rights activism: embeddedness, emotions and social movements. *Annals of the Association of American Geographers,* 96: 342–65.

Bose, P.S. (2007) Dreaming of diasporas: urban developments and transnational identities in contemporary Kolkata. *Topia: Canadian Journal of Cultural Studies,* 17: 111–30.

Bourgois, P. (2003) *In Search of Respect: Selling Crack in El Barrio* (2nd edn). Cambridge: Cambridge University Press.

Burawoy, M., Blum, J.B., George, S., Gille, Z., Gowan, T., Haney, L., Klawiter, M., Lopez, S.H., Ó Riain, S. and Thayer, M. (2001) *Global Ethnography: Forces, Connections, and Imaginations in a Postmodern World.* Berkeley, CA: University of California Press.

Clifford, J. (1986) Introduction: partial truths, in J. Clifford and G.E. Marcus (eds), *Writing Culture: The Poetics and Politics of Ethnography.* Berkeley, CA: University of California Press, pp. 1–26.

Crossa, V. (2009) Resisting the entrepreneurial city: street vendors' struggles in Mexico City's Historic Center. *International Journal of Urban and Regional Research,* 33: 43–63.

Crotty, S. and Bosco, F. (2008) Racial geographies and the challenges of day labor formalization: a case study from San Diego County. *Journal of Cultural Geography,* 25: 223–44.

Datta, A. (2011) 'Mongrel City': cosmopolitan neighbourliness in a Delhi squatter settlement. *Antipode,* 44: 745–63.

DeLyser, D. and Starrs, P.F. (2001) Doing fieldwork: editor's introduction. *Geographical Review,* 91: iv–viii.

Doshi, S. (2011) The politics of persuasion: gendered slum citizenship in neoliberal Mumbai, in R. Desai and R. Sanyal (eds), *Urbanizing Citizenship: Contested Spaces in Indian Cities*. Thousand Oaks, CA: Sage, pp. 82–108.

Duneier, M. (1999) *Sidewalk*. New York: Farrar, Straus and Giroux.

England, K. (1994) Getting personal: reflexivity, positionality, and feminist research. *Professional Geographer*, 46: 80–9.

Geertz, C. (1967) Under the mosquito net. *The New York Review of Books*, 9 (4): 12–13.

Ghertner, A. (2011) Rule by aesthetics: world-class city making in Delhi, in A. Roy and A. Ong (eds), *Worlding Cities: Asian Experiments and the Art of Being Global*. Oxford: Blackwell, pp. 279–306.

Gibson, K. (2011) *Street Kids: Homeless Youth, Outreach, and Policing New York's Streets*. New York: New York University Press.

Gilbert, M. (1994) The politics of location: doing feminist research at 'home'. *Professional Geographer*, 46: 90–6.

Gilmore, R.W. (2007) *Golden Gulag Prisons: Surplus, Crisis, and Opposition in Globalizing California*. Berkeley, CA: University of California Press.

Goodall, H.L., Jr (2000) *Writing the New Ethnography*. Lanham, MD: Altamira Press.

Goode, R.J., Swanson, K. and Aiken, S.C. (2013) From God to men: media and the turbulent fight for Rio's favelas, in G.H. Curti, J. Craine and S. Aitken (eds), *The Fight to Stay Put: Social Lessons through Media Imaginings of Urban Transformation and Change*. Stuttgart: Franz Steiner Verlag, pp. 161–80.

Gowan, T. (2010) *Hobos, Hustlers, and Backsliders*. Minneapolis, MN: University of Minnesota Press.

Hart, G. (2004) Geography and development: critical ethnographies. *Progress in Human Geography*, 28: 91–100.

Herbert, S. (1997) *Policing Space: Territoriality and the Los Angeles Police Department*. Minneapolis, MN: University of Minnesota Press.

Herbert, S. (2000) For ethnography. *Progress in Human Geography*, 24: 550–68.

Heynen, N. (2006) 'But it's alright Ma, it's life, and life only': radicalism as survival. *Antipode*, 38: 916–29.

Hoffman, D. (2008) Rocks: a portrait of Mohammed, in C. Jeffery and J. Dyson (eds), *Telling Young Lives: Portraits of Global Youth*. Philadelphia, PA: Temple University Press, pp. 123–35.

Jackson, P. (1985) Urban ethnography. *Progress in Human Geography*, 9: 157–76.

Katz, C. (1994) Playing the field: questions of fieldwork in geography. *Professional Geographer*, 46: 67–72.

Katz, C. (2004) *Growing Up Global: Economic Restructuring and Children's Everyday Lives*. Minneapolis, MN: University of Minnesota Press.

Kobayashi, A. (1994) Coloring the field: gender, 'race', and the politics of fieldwork. *Professional Geographer*, 46: 73–80.

Koch, N.R. (2010) The monumental and the miniature: imagining 'modernity' in Astana. *Social and Cultural Geography*, 11: 769–87.

Matthews, S.A., Detwiler, J.E. and Burton, L.M. (2005) Geoethnography: coupling geographic information analysis techniques with ethnographic methods in urban research. *Cartographica*, 40: 75–90.

May, J., Wills, J., Datta, K., Evans, Y., Herbert, J. and McIlwaine, C. (2007) Keep London working: global cities, the British State and London's new migrant division of labour. *Transactions of the Institute of British Geographers*, 32: 151–67.

McDowell, L. (1997) *Capital Culture: Gender at Work in the City*. Oxford: Blackwell.

Nast, H. (1994) Women in the field: critical feminist methodologies and theoretical perspectives. *Professional Geographer*, 46: 54–66.

Newman, K. (1999) *No Shame in My Game: The Working Poor in the Inner City*. New York: Russell Sage Foundation and Knopf.

Nietschmann, B. (2001) The Nietschmann syllabus: a vision of the field. *Geographical Review*, 91: 175–84.

Park, R.E. and Burgess, E.W. (1925) *The City*. Chicago, IL: University of Chicago Press.

Proudfoot, J. (2011) The anxious enjoyment of poverty: drug addiction, panhandling, and the spaces of psychoanalysis. PhD dissertation, Simon Fraser University, Burnaby, British Columbia, Canada.

Rodgers, D. (2007) Joining the gang and becoming a broder: the violence of ethnography in contemporary Nicaragua. *Bulletin of Latin American Research*, 26: 444–61.

Ruddick, S. (1996) *Young and Homeless in Hollywood: Mapping Social Identities*. New York: Routledge.

Sparks, T. (2011) Governing the homeless in an age of compassion: homelessness, citizenship, and the 10-year plan to end homelessness in King County Washington. *Antipode*, 44: 1510–31.

Swanson, K. (2008) Witches, children and Kiva-the-research-dog: striking problems encountered in the field. *Area*, 40: 55–64.

Swanson, K. (2010) *Begging as a Path to Progress: Indigenous Women and Children and the Struggle for Ecuador's Urban Spaces*. Athens, GA: University of Georgia Press.

Till, K. (2005) *The New Berlin: Memory, Politics, Place*. Minneapolis, MN: University of Minnesota Press.

Wacquant, L. (2004) *Body and Soul: Notebooks of an Apprentice Boxer*. Oxford: Oxford University Press.

Wills, J., Datta, K., Evans, Y., Herbert, J., May, J. and McIlwaine, C. (2010) *Global Cities at Work: New Migrant Divisions of Labour*. London: Pluto Press.

Wright, M. (2004) From protests to politics: sex work, women's worth and Ciudad Juárez modernity. *Annals of the Association of American Geographers*, 94: 369–86.

6

WORKING IN THE SHADOW ZONES OF URBAN ECONOMIES: USING QUESTIONNAIRES TO RESEARCH HIDDEN POPULATIONS

Nik Theodore

Introduction

One of the challenges facing students who are exploring urban phenomena is selecting appropriate methods for collecting data. The challenge is even greater when the population of interest is difficult to access, and when there is little information on the topic. For example, think about the last time you walked along the streets of a major city and encountered people hawking everything from handbags to tamales, to soft drinks and handmade jewelry. How many vendors are working the streets of this city? How much do they earn on a typical day? And how often do they work each week? The answers to these questions can tell us a lot about the operation of 'invisible' economies that are located in plain sight, yet are often overlooked in the hustle and bustle of urban life. Who are these vendors, and what attracts them to these open-air markets? And what options are available to them other then street vending? It is quite likely that these basic questions have gone unanswered. This means that the field is wide open to students to shed light on various forms of economic activity, if they have carefully chosen their research methods.

Urban economies have never really resembled the markets described in the economics textbooks you may have read, where supply and demand curves conveniently come to rest at an equilibrium point. Instead, they are arenas where business practices collide with institutions of regulation; where job markets are splintered by race, gender, class, age and immigration status; and where roiling competitive dynamics are remaking employment relations on an on-going basis (Castree et al. 2004; Peck 1996; Tilly and Tilly 1998; Wills et al. 2010). Urban labor markets in particular seem to be in a perpetual state of unrest, with employers experimenting with alternative staffing arrangements, extended supply chains, and various forms of subcontracted labor. This in turn has produced new vulnerabilities in the already fractured and fractious labor markets of urban areas.

Since experimentation, competition, and disequilibrium define the messy worlds of urban economies, it should come as no surprise that pockets of disadvantage have been produced at the intersection of employer demand and labor supply. Employers' desires for increased labor flexibility have led to growth in precarious employment, where work schedules are shifting and uncertain, jobs are hazardous, pay levels are low, and job security has been eroded (see Standing 2011). At the sharp end of these transformations are highly casualized jobs, such as those of day laborers, household workers, on-call workers, and street vendors. Here, the rules of regularity and certainty have been replaced by a near-daily struggle to make ends meet. Workers employed in these shadow zones of urban economies routinely suffer violations of basic employment rights, labor standards effectively having been voided by their employers.

From both a policy and research standpoint, the conditions present in these shadow zones remain poorly understood. Workers and the businesses that employ them are located, for all intents and purposes, beyond the reach of government regulation. Likewise, except in rare cases, academic researchers have been unable to fully come to grips with the changes that have occurred. As a result, knowledge gaps exist regarding the working conditions, employment arrangements, and business practices that are present within sectors of urban economies where precarious jobs predominate. This calls for new studies using a range of research methodologies to uncover the underlying conditions present in urban economies, as well as their impacts on workers and communities. Questionnaires are one important part of this larger methodological picture.

This chapter describes the use of questionnaires to collect information from workers who are employed in precarious jobs, who often are neglected or ignored in traditional research studies. Designed to be a guide for students who are planning to use questionnaires in researching the city, this chapter makes specific reference to exploring the changing conditions at the bottom of urban economies. But the advice applies to the use of questionnaires in investigating other urban issues as well. The first section considers the use of questionnaires to investigate conditions in urban economies. This is followed by a set of guidelines for using questionnaires to collect data from workers. The third section illustrates the use of questionnaires by considering a case study of homeless men and women who are employed by day labor temp agencies in Chicago. The final section reviews the strengths and weaknesses of questionnaires as a tool for conducting urban field research.

Entering the field

Studying complex urban phenomena presents numerous challenges concerning access to research subjects and analysis of data that has been collected. As with any research project, it is important for you to think carefully about the objectives of the research and to think ahead about how data will be used. The selection of appropriate research methods is dependent, in large part, on this reflection. But considerations about cost, time, and access also figure prominently in the choice of methods. For those of you interested in investigating conditions in urban labor markets or in areas such as housing, transportation, and use of social services, surveys have been a popular, though time-consuming, method of data collection.

Despite the challenges, questionnaires are an important tool for social inquiry, and they have a crucial role to play in understanding conditions in urban labor markets. Surveys are often used by researchers to collect original data and to describe a population that is too large to observe directly. Using probability sampling (which identifies a subset of the population whose characteristics reflect the larger population) and well-crafted questionnaires, investigators are able to collect data that is representative of the target population. Questionnaires can also be used for exploratory research when hypotheses are being developed, as well as for large-scale surveys that produce statistically representative population estimates and other findings. In the case of contingent workers, surveys have been an important means of conducting exploratory research that documents worker experiences, examines working conditions in an industry, and explores the dynamics of local labor markets. Survey questionnaires have been a key tool for examining changes in employment relations that have been missed by government surveys, business surveys, and conventional employment data – the other types of data you might be considering including in your dissertation.

In the case of labor market researchers, there are at least three reasons why they tend to rely on worker surveys when documenting substandard conditions. First, workers can be a reliable source of information about their own employment experiences and, to a lesser extent, about the experiences of their co-workers. Questions about wages, schedules, job tasks, and injuries are easy for workers to answer directly. In some industries, such as street vending and household work, it is likely that workers are the only reliable source of information about employment conditions. Second, workers are often willing to discuss workplace conditions, even when lengthy questionnaires are used. This means that large amounts of information about labor practices and workplace conditions can be collected. Finally, employers are often reluctant to discuss their own role in downgrading employment conditions. Employer interviews or business case studies might reveal the inner workings of particular firms and the industries of which they are a part, but it is likely that less scrupulous employers will refuse to submit themselves to potential scrutiny. As a result, information about industry practices gathered directly from employers may be skewed in favor of those enterprises that do a better job 'playing by the rules'.

Before proceeding with questionnaire development, piloting, and administration, there are important questions for you to consider. These include:

- Can you accurately identify and access the target population? While there are ways to identify registered voters or participants in a university course, such as the one you are currently on, no such lists exist, for example, of homeless persons, minimum-wage workers, or street vendors.
- Are there geographic impediments to survey administration? Some populations cluster geographically (such as day laborers who search for work in public spaces) while others do not (such as street vendors who may move from location to location). Is the method chosen suitable to the geographic distribution of the target population?
- Will members of the target population participate in the study? Respondents may be unwilling to answer a questionnaire if they believe doing so might compromise their personal safety or well-being. Undocumented immigrants, for example, might be unwilling to participate in a survey because of the fear that doing so might lead to detection by immigration authorities. Additionally, workers in general might be reticent to speak with researchers because they worry that their employers might learn of their participation in the study and respond vindictively.

Once you have considered these questions and determined both that the topic is suitable for examination through the use of a questionnaire and that the target population is accessible, it is time to move on to the task of questionnaire development.

Researching the shadow zones using questionnaires

One of the objectives of studies on emergent forms of labor relations is to explore and document conditions in segments of local economies where employment relations have been fundamentally transformed. However, because conditions are changing, you might find writing effective questions to be difficult. In such cases, you may want to conduct semi-structured interviews with staff at community organizations, workers, or others who have concrete knowledge about working conditions in the industries and occupations of interest. As Cochrane sets out in Chapter 4, there are issues that you will need to consider when using this method. The information collected from these interviews will be a useful guide during the questionnaire-development process, and will ensure that you ask the right people the right questions.

Questionnaire development

Individual questions can be formatted in one of two ways. Close-ended questions ask respondents to choose from a limited number of responses that have been predetermined by the researcher. Close-ended questions might involve the use of true/false constructions, multiple-choice answers, scales (such as those ranging from 'strongly agree' to 'strongly disagree'), numerical responses, or ordinal variables where there is a clear ordering to potential responses (such as 'low', 'medium', 'high'). Close-ended questions are used for quantitative analysis of responses. They will allow you to easily summarize and analyze results across the sample, including the calculation of distributions and averages. When providing lists of potential responses, individual answers should be mutually exclusive, and as a group these responses should cover the range of potential answers to a question (though you will likely include an 'other' option at the end of lists of possible responses). Examples of close-ended questions include, 'In the last week, how many times did you report to the temp agency to look for work?' or 'In the last three years, have you ever suffered an injury on the job that required medical attention?'

Questions that allow respondents to answer in any way they deem appropriate are said to be 'open-ended' because responses are not given in a standardized format and respondents are free to answer in their own words. Examples of open-ended questions include, 'Please describe the type of on-the-job injury you suffered' or 'What happened when you brought a complaint about workplace safety to your employer?' Open-ended questions are especially useful when conducting exploratory research since they provide a means of collecting responses that might not have been anticipated by the investigator at the outset of the research project. However, for large surveys, open-ended questions can be cumbersome to code and analyze, and therefore they should be used sparingly.

The precise wording of questions is an aspect of questionnaire development in which great care must be taken. Questions should be neutral so that respondents are not led, directly or indirectly, to any particular answer. So-called leading questions will result in biased responses. The wording of questions also should be as simple and straightforward as possible, avoiding the use of jargon (like the phrase 'contingent work'!), confusing sentence structures, and double negatives. Questions should inquire into a single topic rather than being 'double-barreled' questions containing more than one part, otherwise you will not know the aspect of the question to which the research subject is responding. One clue that a question might be double barreled is the use of the word 'and' linking two or more potentially different topics in the same question. So, avoid the use of conjunctions when phrasing your questions.

Questions should be arranged in ways that are logical for a respondent. For example, topics should be grouped together when possible, and time periods of events should not shift too much within the questionnaire. Otherwise, respondents may become confused about the exact events or circumstances on which they are being asked to report. For example, if the investigator is trying to collect information about worker injuries on the job along with information on work schedules, it makes sense to group injury questions in one part of the questionnaire and scheduling questions in another part of the questionnaire. In addition, because injuries are (hopefully) relatively rare occurrences, the time period for questions regarding on-the-job injuries can be long ('In the *last three years* have you been injured on the job?'), while scheduling changes might occur frequently ('In the *last week* how may hours did you work for your employer?').

Once a questionnaire is developed and refined, it must be piloted (pre-tested) to ensure that the questions are stated clearly and can be answered by potential respondents. Piloting involves testing the survey on a small number of individuals who are members of the target population. This is a crucial step in the process of questionnaire development since questions must be written in such a way that respondents can truthfully and accurately answer them. Even the most careful researchers will make errors, such as writing ambiguous questions, failing to account for all possible responses, or other mistakes. Questions will need to be re-written in cases where misunderstandings or omissions are found to exist during the pilot phase. Moreover, if you are savvy you will use this step to eliminate questions that have limited usefulness to the final analysis since they pose a cost to the investigator in terms of time, and they are a burden on respondents who are being asked to answer questions with little relevance or purpose.

Administering questionnaires

Questionnaires can be administered to respondents through several different methods, including web-based surveys, mail surveys, telephone surveys, and in-person surveys. This section discusses these methods and considers their relative applicability to researching low-wage, contingent work and accessing hidden populations in general.

Web-based surveys are a low-cost method for collecting responses to relatively straightforward questions. They allow respondents to complete the survey in their own time, at their own pace, and in a location of their choosing. New web-based tools allow investigators to quickly design surveys, compile responses easily, and analyze results. However, web-based surveys also have significant drawbacks: they require respondents to have ready access to computers and to the Internet; they depend on relatively high literacy levels and comfort with information technology; response rates tend to decline with the length of the survey; and they do not allow respondents to ask clarifying questions of interviewers. In addition, the depersonalized nature of web-based surveys may be a barrier for collecting information of a sensitive nature. For these reasons, web-based surveys are not recommended for interviewing low-wage workers or for interviewing hidden populations.

Mail surveys are a means of reaching large numbers of potential respondents. This technique relies on respondents filling out a questionnaire in a timely manner and then to mail the completed questionnaire back to the investigator. Like web-based surveys, mail surveys work best when targeted respondents are highly literate. Likewise, they share some of the drawbacks of web-based surveys: they do not allow respondents to ask clarifying questions; they depend on the willingness of respondents to take the time to independently complete (and then return) the survey; and their administration is depersonalized, and therefore surveying lacks the 'human touch' associated with in-person interviewing. These drawbacks are significant when surveying hidden populations, so mail questionnaires are not recommended for surveying low-wage workers.

Telephone surveys are a popular method for conducting surveys of the general population. With this method, investigators randomly select telephone numbers from a target area, and then administer in-person interviews to respondents. Telephone surveys allow investigators to cover wide geographical areas and, because surveys are conducted in person, clarification about question meaning and intent is possible. However, this method has significant drawbacks when trying to survey low-wage workers. Telephone surveys must be conducted during a narrow call window when respondents are likely to answer the telephone; potential respondents may 'screen' their calls and not answer the telephone; and locating telephone numbers for specific populations, like low-wage workers, may be impossible.

In-person surveys are a fourth method of data collection. In-person surveys involve administering questionnaires directly to respondents. This method offers several advantages to investigators who are trying to document conditions in low-wage labor markets: response rates tend to be high; respondents who are interacting directly with an interviewer may be willing to complete longer, more complex questionnaires; interviewers can screen respondents to ensure they are a part of the target population; interviewers have the opportunity to answer clarifying questions, so response quality may be high; and interpersonal bonds may be established between interviewer and respondent, which in turn may facilitate the collection of sensitive information. This method also has several drawbacks, however, including that it might be time-consuming for the interviewer to complete the requisite number of surveys and that the questionnaires must be administered during times that are convenient for both the interviewer and respondent. On balance, though, in-person surveys are the preferred method for administering questionnaires to workers holding contingent jobs.

Analyzing contingent work

Questionnaires have been an important resource for researchers who are investigating employment and working conditions in the shadow zones of urban economies –

jobs and industries where conditions are substandard, but the jobs themselves and the workers who hold them have largely fallen outside the purview of government agencies and of academic research studies. Since 2000, however, large-scale studies of these 'hidden' populations in the workforce have been conducted in the United States and elsewhere, including surveys of immigrant day laborers (Theodore et al. 2006; Valenzuela et al. 2006), household workers (Burnham and Theodore 2012), street vendors (Goetz and Wolstein 2007; Sluszka and Basinski 2006), taxi drivers (Blasi and Leavitt, 2006; Bruno 2009), warehouse workers (Warehouse Workers for Justice 2010), and low-wage workers in general (Bernhardt et al. 2009). Surveying each of these populations presents its own challenges that can be resolved through different outreach methods, interview sites, and survey protocols. For the purposes of this chapter, the benefits of using questionnaires in urban field research will be elaborated through a study that was undertaken in Chicago regarding the employ-ment experiences of a segment of the local workforce (Theodore 2003). The following case study provides an example of how questionnaires can be used to collect data from one hidden population – homeless adults who are employed by temp agencies.

A fair day's pay?

The Chicago Coalition for the Homeless is an organization that works with homeless men, women, and children to end homelessness by tackling its root causes. Over its 30-year history, the Coalition has advocated for programs and policies to improve access to jobs paying family-supporting wages, to expand the availability of quality health care, and to increase the supply of affordable housing. It also has tried to raise public awareness of the multiple dimensions of homeless-ness, and to that end it has commissioned surveys and other research studies to illuminate aspects of the problem.

At the close of the 1990s, the United States had experienced one of the great-est economic expansions in its history. Yet the problem of working poverty was worsening, while homelessness remained as intransigent as ever. As the Chicago Coalition for the Homeless sought to understand how working Chicagoans are forced into homelessness, it became clear that certain forms of employment were implicated in the deepening of poverty and the perpetuation of homeless-ness. Foremost among these is an employment arrangement commonly known as 'day labor'.

Day labor – working through temporary staffing agencies or waiting on 'labor corners' to secure low-paying, manual-laborer jobs in factories, warehouses, and construction sites is one form of contingent work that appears to be on the rise in US cities (see Peck and Theodore 2001; Reavis 2010; Theodore et al. 2006; Valenzuela et al. 2006). In the USA, much of the market for day workers is organized by temporary staffing agencies that hire workers who are then dispatched to the worksites of other employers on an as-needed basis (Theodore and Peck 2002). Day laborers are employed without the benefits of *any* job security (in fact the length of their employment 'contract' is completely unspecified and at the discretion of the agency and the worksite employer), typically for low wages and without fringe benefits. Most workers queue at the agency each morning in the hope that they will be dispatched to a worksite that day. Supplying workers wherever they are needed, whenever they are needed is the *raison d'être* of the day labor industry. Agencies tend to locate in high-poverty neighborhoods where there are large pockets of underemployed workers with few other opportunities for earning a living, and they rely on unemployed and underemployed workers to fill the ranks of a roaming workforce that is mobilized on a daily basis (Peck and Theodore 2001).

By the 1990s, homeless adults had become an important source of workers for day labor temp agencies in the United States (Kerr and Dole 2005; Parker 1994; Reavis 2010), though the industry itself had received little attention from policymakers, academics, or the media. In Chicago, the staff of the Coalition for the Homeless increasingly received complaints from constituents regarding treatment by temp agencies. Faced with the question of how best to understand and document the relationship between day labor and homelessness, it commissioned a study to explore the employment experiences of homeless adults hired by day labor temp agencies. Researchers began by developing a questionnaire that explored key aspects of respondents' working lives, including their recent employment histories, hourly wages, monthly earnings, use of welfare benefits, concerns about job safety, and demographic characteristics. A team of interviewers was trained to administer the questionnaires in person to residents of four large emergency shelters in Chicago. In keeping with standard survey protocols, interviewers were asked to follow the question wording in the instrument exactly, skipping any questions that a respondent refused to answer. The survey of homeless men and women then was administered to 510 adults at the shelters on a single night. Respondents were given a small stipend of 5 dollars for taking the time to complete the questionnaire.

The survey produced a number of findings, some surprising and some expected. While it was known that day labor temping was an important source of employment for homeless adults, the extent to which homeless individuals were employed by agencies surprised even long-term advocates and community organizers. Fully 75 percent of the sample had held a day labor assignment in the previous 12 months, meaning that day labor is the primary source of employment for these homeless adults. At a time when the minimum wage rate was $5.15 per hour, 82 percent of the sample earned $5.50 per hour or less at their day labor job, while just 0.6 percent earned $8.00 or more per hour. Low wage rates led some workers in our sample to pursue other sources of income, such as selling cans, asking strangers for money, giving blood or plasma, and/or collecting public benefits.

From the work schedules and income data collected, it was possible to develop four scenarios that characterize the earnings of different groups of homeless workers employed by day labor agencies. The survey made clear that homeless day laborers are engaged in a constant struggle to make ends meet. Those with only modest work skills are frequently unemployed or are among the last to receive assignments from their agencies. It was estimated that these workers could earn between $6,000 and $7,000 annually from day labor, as long as they returned to agencies on a regular basis in search of work. Workers with more experience and better work habits could expect to work more often but still would likely find themselves earning annual wages of only about $7,000. These workers will be placed more quickly than their less job-ready counterparts, but given the low pay and unstable working conditions that characterizes day labor, their earnings will remain chronically low. Day laborers who are able to secure steady work while avoiding seasonal downturns could earn between $8,500 and $9,000 per year. If these workers are able to secure occasional assignments paying $7.00 per hour or if they are able to pick up some overtime hours, their annual earnings may climb to $10,000. For reliable workers with experience and strong work habits this is possible to achieve, although clearly even this level of earnings presents considerable hardships for workers. Finally, the most fortunate day laborers who are able to work without interruption while earning wages that are at the top of those typically earned may receive annual pay of between $11,000 and $14,500. Such a scenario was implausible given the insecurity of work and the compression of wages in the industry, so this figure was a marker of the upper limit that a typical day laborer might reasonably hope to earn.

Using data from government publications, these earnings scenarios were then compared to a basic budget composed of average living and work-related expenses for a single adult in Chicago. On the income side were earnings from day labor as well as income from public aid and other sources. It was determined that a worker earning between $6,500 and $8,000 a year from day labor would have a monthly, pre-tax income of between $542 and $667. A common form of income support for single working adults with very low incomes is Food Stamps. At the time, a single low-wage worker in Illinois may be eligible for up to $127 per month in Food Stamps. If the day-laborer worker were to receive the maximum Food Stamp allowance, the worker's income from day labor and food stamps combined would be between $669 and $794 each month. Even when adding in income from alternative sources, it is unlikely that the monthly earnings of homeless day laborers would be much in excess of between $600 and $850. Of course employment taxes would reduce this amount, but for the purposes of the analysis the above figures were not altered.

On the expense side of the budget, the major cost would be rent. The average rent for a studio apartment in Chicago at that time was $820 per month (data from *Chicago Tribune*, 1999). Assuming that the worker was able to rent a studio at two-thirds of the Chicago average rental cost, rent for this worker would be $546 per month. The US Department of Agriculture (USDA) calculates baseline costs of food eaten at home by families of various sizes and budgets. According to USDA, under the 'low-cost plan' the food expenses of a single male aged 20–50 were $185 per month (United States Department of Agriculture 1999). Utilities costs would add an additional $119 per month (United States Bureau of the Census 1996). Transportation by the agencies to work sites would cost the worker an additional $40 per month. Even when leaving the costs of health care, clothing, and personal care out of the equation, the living expenses incurred by the worker would be on the order of $890 per month, well below the likely earnings from day labor and other sources. In short, rather than providing an income that would allow workers to afford the necessities of life, day labor provides the minimum income required for workers to feed themselves and to return to work the next day.

The upshot of this investigation is that although day labor provides income to thousands of homeless men and women in Chicago, allowing them to survive day to day, the very nature of this employment arrangement fosters workers' dependency on low-wage, unstable work. If day labor afforded homeless workers the resources to live in adequate housing, to feed their families, and to build stable careers, day laborers could have the opportunity to escape this dependency. However, day labor provides neither the income nor the employment security necessary for these workers to rise out of homelessness or poverty.

Conclusion

When carefully constructed, tested, and administered, questionnaires can be an important means of data collection. They are potentially useful to explore a variety of urban issues – such as those you may be considering in your dissertation. The survey described in this chapter of homeless adults employed by day labor temp agencies covered a range of other issues that will not be summarized here, including work scheduling, labor standards and violations of employment laws, and information on the characteristics of worksites. These issues illustrate the breadth of issues that can be covered in a questionnaire of moderate length. Worker surveys arguably have been one of the most important methods for documenting fast-changing conditions in urban economies and in shedding light on new sources of worker vulnerability. When combined with other data sources, as was done with the comparison of earnings to basic budgets, the results from questionnaires can provide powerful analyses of contemporary conditions, illuminating the inner workings of local labor markets that too often are obscured, even to seasoned observers.

In short, questionnaires offer you a potentially rich source of original data. Of course they also have their limitations. The requirement that questionnaires are standardized so that respondents are asked the same questions means that surveys are not nearly as flexible as other methods of interviewing that allow respondents greater leeway in answering questions in their own words. Furthermore, questionnaires do not allow investigators to 'go with the flow' of the interview and ask a series of follow up questions after being given an intriguing response. Because of this, the questionnaire might miss important aspects of the condition that is being studied. In these ways, questionnaires 'bracket' elements of context and situation, and when compared to participant observation, diaries, or even in-depth interviewing, they may miss some of the nuances of the lived experience. So, as is the case with any data collection method, the use of questionnaires presents the researcher with a set of tradeoffs. Those of you who intend to use the questionnaire method need to reflect on the kind of data you need in order to answer your research questions (see Chapter 2, this volume). So long as you are aware of what the method can and cannot deliver then you are ideally placed. In my case, the questionnaire, coupled with the use of other research methods and data, allowed me to address my research questions and produce a series of reports and academic articles. The process you will go through to complete your dissertation is similar, and should help to better understand the real-world issues you are exploring.

Frequently Asked Questions

1. When is it appropriate to use survey questionnaires?

Surveys are used by researchers to collect original data and to describe a population that is too large to observe directly. Surveys require researchers to have ready access to population members, and population members must be willing to answer survey questions as completely and honestly as possible. Therefore, the researcher will have to assess whether the research topic is suitable to this form of social inquiry. If the topic involves respondents having to divulge socially unacceptable activities, for example, surveys might not be an appropriate method of data collection.

2. How should I record survey responses?

Surveys can be designed using common word processing programs, spreadsheet programs, or specially designed, online computer programs such as Survey Monkey. Depending on the setting and

(Continued)

(Continued)

the complexity of the survey, responses can be recorded on printed surveys or directly into a computer using software or online tools. When surveying populations that are 'tech savvy', such as fellow students, recording responses directly into a computer might be acceptable. However, in cases where entering responses into a computer might make the respondent feel uneasy, paper surveys are preferable.

3. How can I ensure that the privacy of survey respondents is respected?

It is important that researchers respect the privacy of survey respondents by ensuring that responses are not linked to identifying information, such as name or address. There are several steps you can take to safeguard the anonymity of respondents. These include using a numbering system to catalogue completed surveys, instead of personal identifiers. In addition, surveys typically should be conducted in private, as opposed to in public spaces, in front of co-workers, or in other groups. Respondents should also be notified that if they do not feel comfortable answering any questions, they are free to skip those questions.

4. How can I tell if my questionnaire is too long?

There is no 'correct' length for a questionnaire, but there are a few considerations you will want to keep in mind. If a respondent is not being compensated for the survey or cannot expect to directly benefit from the results of the study, the respondent may not have the patience for a long survey. Perhaps the best measure is for the researcher to adopt the position of the respondent. Does the survey seem too long? Pilot testing the questionnaire can also provide a good guide regarding survey length. Be sure to ask the pilot testers if the survey seemed too long.

5. What type of computer program should I use to analyze my questionnaires?

Simple questionnaires can be tallied using a spreadsheet program. However, if you are interested in running frequencies, computing averages, and producing other descriptive statistics, a statistical program such as SPSS should be used.

Follow Up References

There are a number of helpful textbooks that provide guidance on questionnaire development and survey implementation. These guides tend to cover similar issues: how to use questionnaires, techniques of population sampling, question development, analyzing survey results, and ethical issues when using questionnaires. Popular survey textbooks include:

Fink, A. (2009) *How to Conduct Surveys: A Step-by-Step Guide.* Thousand Oaks, CA: Sage.

Fowler, F.J., Jr (2009) *Survey Research Methods* (4th edn). Thousand Oaks, CA: Sage.

Rea, L.M. and Parker, R.A. (2005) *Conducting Survey Research: A Comprehensive Guide* (3rd edn). San Francisco, CA: Jossey–Bass.

Sapsford, R. (2007) *Survey Research* (2nd edn). London: Sage.

de Vaus, D. (2002) *Surveys in Social Research* (5th edn). London: Routledge.

References

Bernhardt, A., Milkman, R., Theodore, N., Heckathorn, D., Auer, M., DeFilippis, J., Gonzalez, A.L., Narro, V., Perelshteyn, J., Polson, D. and Spiller, M. (2009) *Broken Laws, Unprotected Workers: Violations of Employment and Labor Laws in America's Cities.* Chicago, Los Angeles and New York: UIC Center for Urban Economic Development, UCLA Institute for Research on Labor and Employment, and National Employment Law Project.

Blasi, G. and Leavitt, J. (2006) *Driving Poor: Taxi Drivers and the Regulation of the Taxi Industry in Los Angeles.* Los Angeles, CA: UCLA School of Public Affairs.

Bruno, R. (2009) *Driven into Poverty: A Comprehensive Study of the Chicago Taxicab Industry.* Chicago, IL: University of Illinois School of Labor and Employment Relations.

Burnham, L. and Theodore, N. (2012) *Home Economics: The Invisible and Unregulated World of Domestic Work.* New York: National Domestic Workers Alliance.

Castree, N., Coe, N.M., Ward, K. and Samers, M. (2004) *Spaces of Work: Global Capitalism and Geographies of Labour.* London: Sage.

Goetz, K. and Wolstein, J. (2007) *Street Vending in LA: Promoting Health Eating in LA Communities.* Los Angeles: UCLA School of Public Affairs.

Kerr, D. and Dole, C. (2005) Cracking the temp trap: day laborers' grievances and strategies for change in Cleveland, Ohio. *Labor Studies Journal,* 29: 87–108.

Parker, R.E. (1994) *Flesh Peddlers and Warm Bodies: The Temporary Help Industry and Its Workers.* New Brunswick, NJ: Rutgers University Press.

Peck, J. (1996) *Work-Place: The Social Regulation of Labor Markets.* New York: Guilford Press.

Peck, J. and Theodore, N. (2001) Contingent Chicago: restructuring the spaces of temporary labor. *International Journal of Urban and Regional Research,* 25: 471–96.

Reavis, D.J. (2010) *Catching Out: The Secret World of Day Laborers.* New York: Simon & Schuster.

Sluszka, S. and Basinski, S. (2006) *Peddling Uphill: A Report on the Conditions of Street Vendors in New York City*. New York: Urban Justice Center.

Standing, G. (2011) *The Precariat: The New Dangerous Class*. London: Bloomsbury.

Theodore, N. (2003) Political economies of day labour: regulation and restructuring of Chicago's contingent labour markets. *Urban Studies*, 40: 1811–28.

Theodore, N. and Peck, J. (2002) The temporary staffing industry: growth imperatives and limits to contingency. *Economic Geography*, 78: 463–93.

Theodore, N., Valenzuela, A., Jr and Melendez, E. (2006) *La Esquina* (The Corner): day laborers on the margins of New York's formal economy. *Working USA*, 9: 407–23.

Tilly, C. and Tilly, C. (1998) *Work Under Capitalism*. Boulder, CO: Westwood Press.

United States Bureau of the Census (1996) *Statistical Abstract of the United States, 1995*. Washington, DC: United States Bureau of the Census.

United States Department of Agriculture (1999) Official USDA Food Plans: Cost of Food at Home at Four Levels, US Average, September 1998. Washington, DC: United States Department of Agriculture.

Valenzuela, A., Jr, Theodore, N., Melendez, E. and Gonzalez, A.L. (2006) *On the Corner: Day Labor in the United States*. Los Angeles, CA: UCLA Center for the Study of Urban Poverty.

Warehouse Workers for Justice (2010) *Bad Jobs in Goods Movement*. Chicago, IL: Warehouse Workers for Justice.

Wills, J., Datta, K., Evans, Y., Herbert, J., May, J. and McIlwaine, C. (2010) *Global Cities at Work: New Migrant Divisions of Labour*. London: Pluto Press.

7

DISCOURSE AND LINGUISTIC ANALYSIS

Annette Hastings

Introduction

Researchers who use discourse analysis in their work argue that language matters. They argue that language is not a neutral medium for describing the world, but that its use is caught up in ideology and power relations. They therefore argue that language does not simply refer to or reflect back an independent social world, but that it is somehow involved in producing it or sustaining its characteristics, such as unequal social relations, or the 'identities' available to young people.

Since the time of the Ancient Greeks, the importance of rhetoric and other persuasive forms of language use in political and social life has been well understood. Arguably it is since the mid-1990s that awareness has grown of the effort that goes into managing or 'spinning' the story in politics and policy, as well as understanding of how language is used deliberately and instrumentally to achieve particular effects. Barack Obama, for example, was elected President of the United States in 2008 partly on the back of the slogan *Change we need*. When we think of it now, the strangeness of the word order is striking; it would have been more usual to say *We need change*. But this more conventional word order would not have been helpful to Obama's image or campaign. *We need change* is an abstract proposal – what kind of change do we need? What will it look like?

It is a slogan that provokes uncertainty, confusion, even fear. *Change we need* – in contrast – makes the abstract concrete; we can see what change will look like. Obama's slogan tells us 'I am the change we need', 'This is what change will look like'. Grammatically, what has been done is to switch the object of the sentence so that it becomes the subject of the sentence. In so doing, the nebulousness of the notion of change is transformed – it is quite literally fleshed out in the form of Obama himself.

Language is manipulated in these kinds of ways all of the time. We are all constantly making – more or less constrained – linguistic choices about how to represent ourselves; about how to persuade someone else to do something for us; about how to tell the story of an event to cast ourselves in the best light or to get the biggest laugh. Politicians do it, advertising executives do it, writers such as novelists, journalists and academics do it. And so do the people who will be participating in your research – your interviewees and focus group participants, the authors of the policy documents that you read, and so on.

This chapter should help you build a more critical awareness of the use of language in social and political processes into your dissertation. It will introduce you to some approaches and tools that you can begin to use in your research – like analysing the grammatical transformation identified in Obama's slogan – and show how using these can help augment your understanding of your substantive topic. In this chapter, my examples focus on social regeneration and housing policy. I suggest that such tools can be used by anyone with a sensitivity to language use: someone who is interested or troubled, for example, by the preference of the term 'social exclusion' over 'poverty' and wonders what is at stake when one term gains ascendancy over another. Further, some of the approaches highlighted in this chapter can be combined with many if not all of the research approaches covered in this book. So – even if you don't expect to use discourse or linguistic analysis as a central part of your dissertation – you might still want to read on.

There will be some of you, however, who will not be content simply to 'dabble' with a few tools and techniques of discourse and linguistic analysis. You will want to find out more and to discover why discursive approaches to analysis can be such powerful ways of understanding the connections between texts and talk and wider social processes. Most social scientists who use discourse and linguistic analysis presume that language is fundamentally connected to societal relations. The chapter also aims to provide a brief introduction to these ideas and to signpost those readers who wish to pursue them further to some relevant literature.

In summary then, the aim of this chapter is to encourage you to engage critically with language use in undergraduate and graduate research projects. It aims to help you to incorporate some elements of discourse and linguistic analysis into your work. It argues that it is possible to do this in a range of ways – as just one small aspect of your methodology, as a more substantial element or even as the entire frame underpinning your project.

A brief overview of discourse analysis approaches

There are numerous different approaches to researching the use of language. In some, the purpose is to explain language use with reference to society (for example, sociolinguistics). In others, the aim is to understand society by exploring the role of language (discourse analysis broadly defined). In this chapter we are concerned only with the latter group: with research approaches that start from a social, urban or political problem and try to understand this societal problem better through a focus on language use.

Two main approaches to discourse analysis have been used most often by urban researchers: the discourse analysis inspired by the French social theorist Michel Foucault; and the critical discourse analysis developed by Norman Fairclough and others. These approaches have tended to be used by researchers with an interpretivist approach to social science. For such researchers, researching the social world requires a focus on what situations, experiences and events *mean* for social actors, and how these meanings are critical to how they experience social reality (Geertz 1973/1993; Yanow 2000). Interpretivists can be contrasted with more positivistic researchers who will tend to see social reality as a more stable phenomenon, largely unaffected by the perspectives of the people involved in it. This means that researchers who use discourse analytical approaches also share a broadly constructivist view of the relationship between reality and our knowledge of it. They argue that our understanding of the external world is always a selective, partial construction, the nature of which depends on who we are and the perspective from which we view it. It is not that they necessarily deny that there are real, objective phenomena such as poverty or inequality. However, they are particularly interested in understanding how specific versions of reality can come to be seen as acceptable or natural. This might, for example, question the idea that economic inequality is inevitable.

Foucauldian-inspired discourse analysis

It is from Foucault that we get the idea that there are distinctive, systematic and identifiable 'discourses' that present particular, coherent ways of describing an aspect of the world. Such discourses create a system of knowledge in which only some things can be true and others are necessarily false. One of Foucault's early examples was to explore how our understandings of 'madness' are dependent and constrained by the social and cultural forces in play at any particular time. He shows how, over time, 'madness' has been variously believed to be caused by an alliance with dark forces, social deviance, or as an illness that can be treated (Foucault 1963/2001). Essentially this idea suggests that discourse is involved in producing a version of reality (events, processes, relations, etc.) and that other versions are always possible, although they may be hidden from view. One role for discourse analysis research is simply to draw attention to the contingency of specific discourses (that is, that they come from a particular perspective) by bringing into view alternative ways of conceptualizing the world.

Foucauldian discourse analysis tends to use a fairly broad-brushed approach to linking language use with social processes. Crucially, it is not always grounded in actual texts or examples of language use. And it does not tend to provide a set of tools that can be used by researchers to analyse actual instances of text and talk, and then to link these insights to a broader understanding of larger macro or historical processes. Rather, it draws attention to the role of language in structuring what can be thought, said or believed in a particular place or time. Finally, Foucault's work was largely underpinned by the idea that language use is shaped by, or even simply reflective of, power relations. Most other approaches to discourse analysis posit a more complex, recursive relationship between language and power, arguing in particular that it can be used to resist the exercise of power. (In later life Foucault apparently did recognize the role of discursive struggles, but he never worked the theoretical point through; Fischer 2003: 40.)

Given that the focus of this chapter is on how we might directly research how language is used in the settings in which we are interested, we leave Foucauldian discourse analysis here. The remainder of the chapter focuses on the other main approach highlighted earlier: critical discourse analysis.

Critical discourse analysis: approach and research tools

The starting point of any critical discourse analysis (CDA) is a social problem or issue – examples might be anti-social behaviour or global warming. Think about your own dissertation interests. Analysis focuses on examining texts in order to understand how these issues or problems are related to power relations in society. Anti-social behaviour could, for example, be revealed to be a consequence of unequal power relations between different social groups (young people and adults, for example). Global warming might be analysed as an outcome of power relations between the more or less developed world, or between political and scientific institutions. CDA therefore shares similar concerns with critical social science generally, but where it differs is in the extent to which it places language and discourse practices at the centre of the processes that reproduce and sustain power and dominance (see Fairclough 2003 for a fuller discussion of its socio-political stance). Therefore, those who practise CDA attempt to link the micro details of texts (wording, grammar, etc.) to wider structural processes, such as the conditions under which some texts rather than others are produced, as well as to larger structures and patterns of language use. Questions of power and inequality guide all aspects of the analysis (Fairclough 2003). In this way, CDA provides a framework for assessing *why* a particular text matters, as well as *how* it makes itself matter – for example, where it gets its authority and credibility from. And it can do this via a fine-grained analysis of words and grammar conducted in relation to broader socio-political analysis.

These ideas are quite difficult. However, they do not require to be understood in detail before deciding to pay more attention to language use in your research projects. At the end of this chapter further references are provided for those who wish to pursue the theoretical side of discourse analysis. However, one theoretical point is worth emphasizing here. We have already said that discourse as a concept implies a strong link between language use and social processes and practices. CDA contends that discourses and their means of communication are intimately related. The argument is that a discourse is concretized in a 'text'; it is in texts that discourses are made real – we can find them there. It is not then simply that texts are the means by which discourses are reproduced and sustained, but that texts give us access to what a discourse makes us think, as well as how it makes us think it. It is this theoretical point – that texts are instantiations of discourses – that provides a rationale for subjecting them to detailed analysis. Some of the examples of analysis provided below might help you connect textual analysis with broader social analysis.

And finally a practical point: what do we mean by texts? In common usage, as well as in social science more generally, a text is usually a sustained piece of written communication – it could be a newspaper article, a book chapter such as this, or a political treatise. However, for the purposes of textual analysis, a much broader definition of text is possible. Texts can be understood as all kinds of communicative events. These might be realized linguistically (conversations, interviews, meetings) or by means of other symbolic systems, so that photographs, organizational uniforms and even buildings can be analysed for the meanings they make and the consequences of these. For a researcher, CDA therefore opens up opportunities to focus on a very broad range of social artefacts in order to develop their understanding of a particular social issue.

Doing discourse analysis: some useful analytical tools

The first step to getting started in doing discourse analysis is to sensitize yourself to language use. This will inevitably involve reading your texts (e.g. policy documents, interview transcripts) critically or sceptically. It might mean reading between the lines – thinking about whether there is a hidden message or subtext – as well as considering what linguistic choices have been made in the production of the text: 'Why say it this way and not another?', 'Who is the author trying to convince and why?'

Social scientists in the interpretivist tradition ask these kinds of questions of their data all the time. Not all of them explicitly use discourse analysis to help them work out the answers. However, there are some relatively easy-to-use approaches and tools that can make the processes and outcomes of engaging critically with language use much more transparent.

Examine words and numbers

A good place to start is to examine the vocabulary used by a speaker or in a written text. We tend to notice the words that people use, partly because there are usually alternative wordings which could have been used. Why, for example, might a government policy document describe the rate of teenage pregnancies in Great Britain as 'shameful' and leading to 'shattered lives and blighted futures' (Cabinet Office 1999: 1). Clearly, emotive language such as this can produce strong effects. It will orientate the reader or listener to evaluate the phenomenon under considera- tion in a particular way. It is notable that in the text quoted here – an introduction to a policy document by the then prime minister, Tony Blair – that the term 'baby' is never used, even though the policy issue in question is teen pregnancy rates, the product of which is babies. Clearly, the term 'baby' will tend to provoke a positive emotional response, which would confuse the message of the document that teen pregnancy rates are harmful and shameful.

One approach to linguistic analysis that focuses on word use is content analysis. Content analysis takes a largely quantitative and systematic approach to exploring patterns in language use, for example, the frequency with which certain words or phrases occur in specific kinds of texts. Content analysis has not been used a great deal to research the city. This is likely to be because the majority of urban research- ers interested in using discourse analysis have tended to come from the qualitative rather than quantitative research traditions (and, as we have seen in the preceding discussion, there is a close alignment between constructivism and discourse analysis, which means a tendency to reject the positivism often, although not always, asso- ciated with quantitative research).

However, recent developments in corpus linguistics (an approach related to con- tent analysis) should not be rejected by researchers interested in language use. Corpus linguistics makes use of new computer software and databases to perform more detailed and sophisticated statistical tests on the wordings of texts. Analysis can be done on the content of specific kinds of texts: for example, on which newspapers tend to put the words 'rampant' together with 'immigration'. Enormous databases of language usage now exist – such as *WordBanks online* – which store many millions of words of English text and allow the patterns within specific texts to be bench- marked and evaluated with reference to a wider 'world of texts'. (Is 'rampant' always pejorative? Does the collocation 'rampant immigration' only occur in certain kinds of text?) Although it is unlikely that many of you would want to use corpus linguistics in your projects, it is useful to be aware of the possibilities for new approaches to studying language use that are being opened up by advances in informatics.

Finally, it is also important to recognize that numbers as well as words can be used strategically to provoke particular emotions. Consider, for example, the extract below from a Scottish policy document concerned with launching a new urban regeneration initiative. In this document the speed of population growth in Glasgow in the late nineteenth and early twentieth centuries is put forward as part of the explanation for the city's contemporary problems:

> Towns and cities grew dramatically as people flocked to them … Nowhere was this more apparent than in Glasgow where the population rose from 500,000 in 1871 to 750,000 in 1891 and topped 1,000,000 in 1914. (Scottish Office 1988: 6)

We will all be familiar with the technique used here to persuade us that a number is (almost unimaginably) large: the numeric representation of '1,000,000' always seems larger than the non-numeric 'one million', for example. Arguably, a million is in itself a number that provokes emotion or feeling; we talk of millionaires for a reason, and the fact that the extract highlights the achievement of a one million population level is no accident either.

There are some additional linguistic devices being used in this extract to persuade the reader of the magnitude of the problem described. For example, there is rhetorical three-part structure to the second sentence (of the sort you might expect to find in a political speech). Thus the trajectory of population growth is described in terms of three stages, which together build towards the climax 'topped 1,000,000'. I have argued in a more detailed, contextualized analysis of this extract that the effect of this structure is to suggest uncontrollable growth, leading to some kind of disaster (Hastings 1998). Part of the argument made in support of this is that the extract portrays Glasgow as an 'extreme case'. Thus, it tells us that while towns and cities in general were growing dramatically at the time, '*nowhere* was this more apparent than in Glasgow'. The extreme-case formulation is part of the way in which the extract seeks to convince the reader to arrive at a particular conclusion. (Note: linguists argue that extreme-case formulations are used when the speaker or writer is in an adversarial situation, or expects not to be believed; by making the claim that they are *completely innocent*, rather than *innocent* to suggest that they are more than usually innocent.)

Finally, we can expose the persuasive wording and structure of the extract by offering an alternative wording. The second sentence could be reworded as follows:

> The populations of all towns and cities were growing dramatically. This was particularly the case in Glasgow where the population doubled between 1871 and 1914.

It should be clear that this alternate wording does not change the basic information provided in the extract, but that its emotive, persuasive power is diminished. Try reading the extracts out loud and test if you feel differently when you read each. If so, this is a clue that you are being orientated to evaluate the information provided in a different manner in each case.

Examining the words and numbers used by speakers and writers is a research strategy open to all. The rewording of prominent sentences and phrases can be attempted by researchers whether or not they have a deeper appreciation of discourse analysis or a linguistic training. It can be a very useful technique for exposing the perspective or persuasiveness of a text. In the rest of this section, a brief outline of some more complex analytical techniques is provided. These generally require the researcher to invest some considerable time in getting to grips with some linguistic categories and ideas.

Grammatical analysis: nominalization and passivization

Nominalization and passivization are grammatical strategies that involve the trans-formation of verbs or activities into nouns. Our understanding of what is at stake in the processes of nominalization and passivization owes much to the work of Roger Fowler and colleagues, particularly their 1979 text *Language and Control*. Fowler argued that these strategies have ideological uses. Using examples from newspaper headlines, he showed how headlines can present situations in particular ways. A key example was his analysis of a news story that reported police violence against protestors. The headline could have been 'Police attack protestors'. However, the formulation 'Attack on protesters' was used. This is an example of nominaliza-tion and passivization: the verb 'attack' is nominalized (turned into a noun) and in so doing the agent conducting the attack (in this case, police officers) is deleted. Fowler argues that these kinds of transformations are not random events but are an ideological choice that deserves notice. (At this point you might want to think again about the transformation involved in Obama's slogan discussed at the beginning of this chapter.)

Fowler also argued that nominalization had further effects. By rendering processes as 'things' they become naturalized as entities within social reality, the existence of which cannot be contested. The most obvious example of this is the widespread use of the noun 'market forces' to refer the activities of human agents buying, selling and exchanging in an economic sense. And, further, these nominalized activities can then be viewed as agents themselves (for example, market forces *demand* that x occurs). This further obscures that human agents are involved in this process, agents who might potentially be involved in shaping a different kind of social reality.

Assumptions and intertextuality

An important aspect of CDA is to explore the intertextuality of a text: that is, the nature and extent to which other texts are referred to or implied in the particular text under scrutiny. The analysis might focus on exploring how an individual text incorporates elements of other texts (for example, direct quotes, summaries or rewording of other texts). The researcher might then consider how, why and with what effect snatches of other texts appear or are used within the text. At a straight-forward level, the analysis might consider how the inclusion of snatches of other texts legitimates an argument or assertion. At a more sophisticated level, the focus might be on questions of hegemony or ideology. It might consider how the con-nections between texts allow what is said in this text to appear to have a wider salience or credibility – for example, how the particularities of identity, interest or whatever in the text appear as universal 'truths'.

A key theoretical point underpinning the notion of intertextuality is that it brings to the fore how texts are connected to each other via what Fairclough (2003: 40) calls the 'world of texts'. Analysing intertextuality is to recognize that all texts are in dialogue with other texts – a text is not authored by a unique, single author, but multi-authored in that it inevitably incorporates ideas, linguistic formulations and so on from other texts. Sometimes this is explicitly recognized – when one author quotes or cites another for example – but more usually it is left unrecognized and unacknowledged. The notion of intertextuality draws attention to the importance of what aspects of other texts are incorporated where, and it also forms a theoretical basis for examining what is not said or the silences within texts. Why does a text fail to incorporate specific other texts and what are the implications when it does? What different voices, ways of seeing, or understandings of the world are left out or excluded?

Intertextuality can also be linked to questions about how texts work in relation to assumptions: how they generate, presuppose, imply and maintain assumptions. Again Fairclough (2003) is helpful in this regard. He argues that texts are destined to make assumptions, as what is said in a text is always 'against a background of what is "unsaid" but taken as given' (2003: 40). The ways in which the linguistic strategies within texts rely on and perpetuate assumptions – and the implications of this – can be illustrated by two papers in the urban and housing research field.

First Hastings' (1998) examination of a Scottish policy document shows how, in order for the reader to make sense of the central argument in the document (that poor populations cause urban problems) the reader needs to supply prior assumptions. In other words, to read the document as coherent – as making sense – prior assumptions from the world of texts about urban problems need to be brought to bear. Fairclough argues that this is no accident. He argues that texts perform ideological work – that they generate *and* maintain discourses about how social reality is and why – by requiring readers to make inferences and assump-tions as they make sense of the texts before them (Fairclough 1992: 177). In a similar vein, Matthews' (2010) analysis of a (different) Scottish policy document explores how it makes use of enthymemes, that is, rhetorical devices where it is assumed that the audience has the (prior) knowledge necessary to complete the logic of the argument. The analysis shows how whole paragraphs operate as enthymemes as the arguments within them only make sense with recourse to an external 'knowledge'; for example, that economic capital gives an individual more of the social capital they need to play a role in sustaining civil society communities (Matthews 2010: 14–15).

Narrative analysis

A final, very useful approach to discourse analysis involves examining the stories told by research participants or in policy documents and processes. Although narrative analysis has its roots in literary criticism and history – the arts and humanities rather than social sciences – it is becoming increasingly popular in policy analysis and political science, particularly among researchers interested in how meaning is made between actors (see Fischer 2003). As might be expected, narrative analysis aims to bring out the nature and content of the stories that are used to explain complex events, interactions and even emotions. A key argument is that human actors are constantly engaged in story telling both as means to aid their own understanding of an aspect of social reality, but also to help other actors form an understanding of it – usually in line with their own view of it (Wagenaar 2011). Story-telling can be conscious and subconscious, but it is almost always strategic and intent on being persuasive. Examples abound in everyday life. Think about how you explain to a friend how you came to be late for your appointment with them. You would most likely embark on a story that might place you as unwitting victim of circumstance, who tried heroically to get there in time against the odds. It's rare for any of us to admit that we simply missed the bus!

Those interested in using narrative analysis to understand policy processes might usefully read the work of Deborah Stone (Stone 1989). She argues that policy interventions tend to have particular, predictable plotlines that lead 'ineluctably' from a policy problem defined in a particular way to a credible, even inevitable solution. In Hastings (1998) I use Stone's notion of plotline to examine how the Scottish Government scripted the process of urban decline – with heroes and villains, tragedies and success stories – in a way that made the intervention devised by the government (in this case 'joined up' partnership working) seem not only sensible, but positively inevitable. Fischer's more recent book (2003) is also helpful for breaking down and exposing how narratives work and the importance of understanding this.

Conclusion: How does discourse analysis help us research the city?

Urban researchers have been using discourse analysis to gain insight into social and political issues since the latter half of the 1990s at least. A key driver for this development has been an increasing tendency for reflexivity (that is, reflection about the impact of our own perspective or position on what we see or think) within research about its role and purpose, particularly with regard to how research knowledge interacts with the policy process. Fopp (2009) asked how the use of language in academic research contributes to shaping a more general understanding of why and how homelessness occurs. He suggests that the metaphors which housing researchers use to explain the causes and dynamics of homelessness are at odds with the actual experience of homelessness. He argues specifically that metaphors such as homeless 'careers' and 'pathways' can inadvertently contribute to an understanding of homelessness as a process that is driven by individual choices and failures, rather than by structural inequalities.

So one way in which using discourse analysis can help us to research the city is that it should sensitize us to language use more generally. How others use language is important, but so is how we use language as researchers. Not everyone who reads this book will go on and use discourse analysis as an explicit method in their research (although I hope that some of you will!). However, all of us can be a bit more aware of how our own use of language can affect the process and outcome of a research project – how we frame our research agenda for example, or how the wording in our survey instruments or interview guide orientates the research participant to answer in a particular way. And we should also be aware that how we write up the research matters – we may not realize just how much persuasive work we put in to our writing. Reflexivity is therefore required to ensure that it manages to remain true to what we have found.

Frequently Asked Questions

1. Do you need special training to do discourse analysis?

You don't need special training in linguistics or any other subject to get started with discourse analysis. Anyone who finds themselves asking questions of texts such as 'Why say it that way?', 'Who is it trying to persuade, and about what?' or 'Why is this group attached to this phrase?' can attempt to answer them without a detailed background in linguistic techniques. You should read round the topic, however, before getting started. The follow up references should help with this.

2. When is discourse analysis an appropriate method?

Discourse analysis is at its most appropriate for research questions that ask about meaning – particularly how meaning is made in

(Continued)

(Continued)

particular ways and for whom. Discourse analysis is also a way of getting a handle on what people do with language – how they signal who they are with it or how they use it to persuade others to their own point of view. Discourse analysis is only appropriate if you care about what language does or how it works.

3. What kinds of texts can be examined using discourse analysis?

All sorts of texts can be examined using discourse analysis. These could be written texts of all kinds. A number of discourse analysts look at the policy documents produced by governments, but you could also examine press releases, websites or transcripts of speeches. You can also use discourse analysis to examine the transcripts you produce from your interviews and focus groups. Discourse analysis is fundamentally interested in exposing how meaning is made via social artefacts. You could therefore examine a page from a newspaper, including photographs, layout and font from this perspective if you wanted!

4. What does discourse analysis add?

When done properly, discourse analysis gives us a new perspective on aspects of the social world which we take for granted. It can help to expose that our understandings of what is normal or inevitable about the social world, such as levels of inequality, are only one version of what is possible. It can also give us insight into how language use – particularly by those who are powerful – leads us to think about things in a particular way.

5. Can discourse analysis be combined with other methods?

Definitely! In fact, one of the key proponents of discourse analysis, Norman Fairclough, argues that if we want a rounded picture of the social world then we should try to combine this approach with others. You could combine it with interviews and focus groups, or with photography and video. There is no one best way to understand the social world, and we often get more insight if we combine perspectives.

Follow Up References

Burr, V. (1995) *An Introduction to Social Constructionism*. London: Routledge.

This is an engaging and very accessible introduction to the philosophical view of the relationship between human actors and social reality which underpins the work of many discourse analysts. If you are not already familiar with social construction-ist perspectives, this is the place to start.

Fairclough, N. (2003) *Analysing Discourse: Textual Analysis for Social Research*. London: Routledge.

This book has been written by one of the leading exponents of critical discourse analysis and is designed to introduce it to social scientists with little previous experience or understanding of the field. It provides a relatively accessible guide to some of the theoretical background to critical discourse analysis and, via a series of chapters, discusses the rationale for a number of different aspects of discourse analysis, as well as examples of how to do them in practice.

Hastings, A. (1998) Connecting linguistic structures and social practices: a discursive approach to social policy analysis. *Journal of Social Policy*, 27: 191–211.

My own paper may be useful for those of you interested in urban 'problems' in particular and how you can use discourse analysis to question the versions of these problems that politicians or the media construct. The paper provides some theoretical background to discourse analysis and then goes step-wise through an actual analysis of an extract from a policy document. It should help you get a sense of what discourse analysis in action looks like.

Stone, D. (1988) *Policy Paradox and Political Reason*. Glenview, IL: Scott Foresman.

I really like this book. It revealed to me the importance of narrative and story-telling in the making of policy – showing that the policy process is as full of heroes and villains, predictable plotlines, and beginnings and endings as any novel. It is rather old now, though, and if you cannot get hold of it, Barbara Czarniawska's more recent book (*Narratives in Social Science Research*, London, Sage, 2004) on using narrative analysis in social science research is very useful.

Wodak, R. and Krzyzanowski, M. (eds) (2008) *Qualitative Discourse Analysis in the Social Sciences*. Basingstoke: Palgrave Macmillan.

This edited collection is written for students new to discourse analysis. It has chapters from a range of experts in the field which introduce students to approaches and techniques that can be used to analyse a range of texts from TV documentaries, newspapers and new media to political rhetoric. There are also very useful chapters on how to analyse your interviews and focus groups from this perspective, and a chapter which explores how to use discourse analysis in ethnographic research projects.

References

Cabinet Office (1999) *Teenage Pregnancy*. Command Paper. London: Cabinet Office.

Fairclough, N. (1992) *Discourse and Social Change*. Cambridge: Polity Press.

Fairclough, N. (2003) *Analysing Discourse: Textual Analysis for Social Research*. London: Routledge.

Fischer, F. (2003) *Reframing Public Policy: Discursive Politics and Deliberative Practices*. Oxford: Oxford University Press.

Fopp, R. (2009) Metaphors in homelessness discourse and research: exploring 'pathways', 'careers' and 'safety nets'. *Housing, Theory and Society*, 26: 271–91.

Foucault, M. (1963/2001) *Madness and Civilization: A History of Insanity in the Age of Reason*. London: Routledge.

Fowler, R., Hodge, B., Kress, G. and Trew, T. (eds) (1979) *Language and Control*. London: Routledge and Kegan Paul.

Geertz, C. (1973/1993) *The Interpretation of Cultures*. New York: Basic Books.

Goffman, E. (1986) *Frame Analysis. An Essay on the Organization of Experience*. Boston, MA: Northeastern University Press.

Hastings, A. (1998) Connecting linguistic structures and social practices: a discursive approach to social policy analysis. *Journal of Social Policy*, 27: 191–211.

Matthews, P. (2010) Mind the gap? The persistence of pathological discourses in urban regeneration policy. *Housing, Theory and Society*, 27: 221–40.

Scottish Office (1988) *New Life for Urban Scotland*. Edinburgh: Scottish Office.

Stone, D. (1989) Causal stories and the formation of policy agendas. *Political Science Quarterly*, 104: 281–300.

Wagenaar, H. (2011) *Meaning in Action: Interpretation and Dialogue in Policy Analysis*. Armonk, NJ: M.E. Sharpe.

Yanow, D. (2000) *Conducting Interpretive Policy Analysis*. Thousand Oaks, CA: Sage.

8

USING DIARIES TO STUDY URBAN WORLDS

Alan Latham

Introduction

Cities buzz with the rhythms of everyday life. The flow of traffic, the back and forth of commuters between home and office, the pulsing of millions of phone calls through copper and fibre-optic cables. The dropping off and picking up of children, to day-care, to school, to endless clubs and extracurricular lessons. The rhythm of meal times ... breakfast, dinner, lunch, brunch, tea, supper. They reverberate to the step, step, step, of thousands upon thousands of people going about their business, to the chatter and noise of socializing, the joy of celebration. Night drifts to day, morning into afternoon, evening into night. The question confronting urban researchers is how can we begin to take account of all these rhythms – all this movement, all this activity?

Well of course social scientists have an arsenal of methods through which to begin to make sense of a city's rhythm. We can simply observe what goes on. We can try to immerse ourselves within the urban environment. We can even try to become what the urban philosopher Lefebvre (2004: 21) called rhythmanalysts. The kind of researcher who 'calls on all his senses'. The rhythmanalyst 'thinks with his body, not in the abstract, but in lived temporality'. Certainly there is something to this kind of naturalistic observational work. But it has limitations. It is immensely time-consuming. It also raises all sorts of puzzling questions about the perspective generated through such observation. To address these questions, we could try to formalize the ways such observations are carried out. Or configure the process of observation – as ethnographers do – as a form of learning through participation (Chapter 5, this volume). We might also think of using more conventional social scientific research techniques like questionnaires (Chapter 6, this volume), or interviews (Chapter 4, this volume), perhaps even focus groups, to get people to tell us about the day-to-day rhythms in which they are enfolded. These techniques might generate more recognizable research material than that produced through the bodily immersed rhythmanalyst. But they also stand removed from the everyday life and rhythms that interest urban researchers. Diaries can offer a productive tool to bridge this gap. Explaining how they help us to do so, how they aid urban researchers think with the mundane, routine, what the writer Georges Perec called the 'infra-ordinary', is the purpose of this chapter (Becker 2007).

This chapter presents a brief overview of some of the ways urban researchers have used diaries. It is made up of six sections. The first introduces diaries as a research method within urban studies. The second explains why researchers have been drawn to using diaries. Section three surveys a range of diary styles that have been used recently by urban researchers. Section four provides practical advice on organizing a diary-based research project. The fifth section presents a description of how GPS and web-based social networking technologies have been used as virtual diaries. The final section considers the limitations of diaries as an urban method.

Diaries as a research technique

Diaries have been used in at least three distinctive ways in urban studies. In the form of travel and activity diaries they have been used to study how and when people move about cities. More qualitatively inclined researchers have used a range of solicited respondent diaries to gather data about how urban environments are inhabited. Solicited diaries may be written, photographic, or involve some combination of both. Most recently, a number of technologically orientated urban scholars have collected people's spontaneous diarizing on social networking platforms such as Twitter, Facebook and online blogs. These have been used to map things as diverse as a city's rhythms of happiness, to intensities of virtual communication across urban space. It should also be noted that urban historians have drawn extensively on diaries as sources of archival accounts of everyday city life in earlier times. The use of such material is covered in this chapter.

Why use diaries to study cities?

We have already seen that there are a range of different ways that might be used to generate research material that explores the rhythms and textures of day-to-day urban life. However, doing research that focuses on the mundane detail of everyday urban routines presents the social researcher with two distinctive problems that conventional techniques such as simple observation, interviews, questionnaires, participant observation and focus groups are not well equipped to deal with. The first of these problems relates to the ability of those being researched to accurately recall past activities. The second problem involves the difficulty of effectively observing interactions that are widely distributed across time and place. It is worth considering these problems in turn.

Routines and the problem of recalling activities that have already happened

Interviews, questionnaires and focus groups are great at generating material about people's general actions and characteristics – what kind of jobs people do, what they think about a particular place, whether they think such and such a policy is fair or reasonable, or why a family chose to live in a particular neighbourhood and not another one. These techniques are less good at reliably pinning down how often a person might undertake a certain activity during a week or a month. Nor do they necessarily provide particularly good accounts of how different activities are sequenced. If a researcher is interested in travel patterns, say, they may also want to know when trips to work get combined with food provisioning, or with childcare, or socializing. This issue of sequencing is not just a problem for transport researchers. Researchers interested in neighbourhood cohesion might want to know how often people interact with others from a different socio-economic background and within what context. They might want to know when during the week these interactions are more common and when less so. An urban public health researcher may need to know when, where and with whom the consumption of harmful substances takes place. They may very well also want to know how such consumption relates to more usual routines of eating and drinking.

The problem we are facing here is not with the techniques *per se* but with the task the researcher is setting those being researched. It is unreasonable to expect people to reliably remember the frequency and ordering of activities that they usually carry out routinely and without a great deal of thought. Ask yourself, for example, whether you could write a list of every item you have purchased this week? If you *could* produce a list that is more or less reliable then ask yourself whether you could also list the time and location where each item on your list was bought. On top of that, could you write down what you were doing before and after you made every transaction? Unless you have an exceptional memory (and most people do not) – or really do not spend very much money – you will most likely find it hard, if not impossible, to produce a list that is accurate. And if you have managed to produce a complete list, in all likelihood you would have had to cheat through referring to your personal organizer, diary, or online bank statement.

The difficulty of observing mundane interactions distributed across time and place

So, the first problem of researching everyday routines and rhythms is about the general as opposed to the specific recall of a respondent's social practice. The second problem has two elements. It is difficult to get people to reflect upon much mundane social action ('it just happens!') and it seems silly to ask 'How does it happen?'. And for any individual or group, the action that the researcher is interested in studying may well be widely distributed temporally and spatially. Say, for example, a researcher is interested in how people interact in a local shopping precinct (as social cohesion researchers might be). It is unlikely that respondents will be able to tell the researcher much about how social interactions take place within that space beyond broad generalities. Indeed it is likely that in many cases people will simply not notice that they are involved in certain kinds of interactions at all. In the supermarket they may fail to notice the way they keep to the left in aisles, or that they tend to defer to older women (or not). People will overlook the fact that they smile a hello at the cashier where they buy their morning coffee, or that they always eat their lunch at a particular spot, or that lunch always – or nearly always – consists of the same thing. (People are often shocked when they realize the degree that their lives are entrained in particular routines and rituals of behaviour.)

How can the urban researcher get around this problem? Eager readers of earlier chapters might respond that ethnography might be a good way of generating research material about these sorts of mundane, barely noticed, widely distributed social actions. And certainly it would if the researcher has a great deal of time and her research subjects are tolerant of her constant presence. Unless the researcher follows an individual through a whole day, participant observation will be largely silent about how the observed interactions fit into people's wider routines and daily commitments. While some researchers have undertaken to follow their respondents through the routines of their day (see Laurier and Philo 2003), this involves very significant commitments from both the researcher and the research respondent. There is a further problem. If the respondent being shadowed actually spends relatively little time involved in the activity being researched, participant observation might prove to be a hugely inefficient (if very rigorous) research strategy.

Diaries can offer ways around the twin problems of recall and distributed mundane action. A diary is essentially a series of written notes of some aspect of the respondent's life kept systematically over a period of time. A diary might be about a relatively narrow aspect of their life, about someone's journey to work, or what food they eat and when. Or it can be relatively all-encompassing. It might be about the social lives of university students, how an individual interacts with others in public spaces, or it might try to track an individual's movement over an extended period of time. Because diaries require that their writers note their action whilst undertaking it, or very soon thereafter, well-designed diaries generate more detailed, more reliable and often more focused accounts of people's mundane, routine, actions than other methodologies. In effect the diary becomes a proxy for the eyes and ears of the researcher. Through using diaries the accurate re-tracing-out of someone's day, week, or month, or whatever period of time does not require the constant presence of the researcher. Instead the diary allows the researcher to virtually accompany her or his research respondent as they go about their day-to-day routines without the intrusiveness and heavy time demands that physically shadowing a respondent would involve.

The kinds of diaries used by urban researchers

Urban researchers have used diaries to study a wide range of different phenomena and in doing so they have approached diaries in quite diverse ways. Some researchers have employed diaries as a stand-alone method. Others have thought of diaries as a tool that needs combining with data generated through other research instruments such as surveys, interviews, or ethnographic observation. That said, broadly speaking there have been two principal ways research respondent diaries have been produced in urban studies. The first are activity diaries or logs and travel diaries. This form of diary has been popular with quantitative researchers wanting either to map the spatial and temporal parameters of a certain activity, or to develop mathematical models about those activities. The second are solicited written and photographic diaries. Obviously, activity diaries are (generally) also written, but here 'written' refers to the fact that respondents are asked to include more impressionistic material along with more quantitative information about time and place.

Activity diaries and travel diaries

An activity diary or a travel diary is simply a log where respondents are asked to systematically record their activity over a given period of time. At their most straightforward such diaries simply involve collecting a diary of one day's activity as part of a more extensive survey of the respondent's life. With activity and travel diaries researchers strictly define the detail and structure of the information to be provided by the respondent within his or her individual diary (see Figures 8.1 and 8.2). A great deal of transportation and mobility research uses material generated in this way. A good recent example is Fan et al.'s (2011) use of single-day diary logs to explore the relationship between commuting patterns and neighbourhood characteristics in the Triangle area in North Carolina. The use of such activity diaries is by no means restricted to transportation researchers. In a study examining how families in Singapore managed life in high-rise flats, Appold and Yuen (2007) based their work on 24-hour diaries. Brown et al. (2008) combined a household survey with one-day activity diaries in their study of the relationship between neighbour types and obesity. Boarnet et al. (2011) similarly used single-day activity diaries to study the effectiveness of retrofitting suburbs to encourage walking. The advantages of using single-days diaries is that they provide the kind of detailed temporal and spatial data needed for high-quality quantitative analysis without placing an onerous burden on research respondents. The downside, of course, is that large numbers of respondents need to be recruited to generate enough material for such analysis. This is especially the case where research is not only concerned with activities on a particular day – say work-week travel patterns – but also with the variations of those activities across longer durations such as a week, or a season.

Other researchers, however, have taken a more temporally ambitious approach to activity diaries. Axhausen and colleagues (Axhausen et al. 2002; Cirillo and Axhausen 2006) in their research into travel patterns have successfully got respondents to complete six weeks of activity diaries. In general it is not necessary to aim for such extended diaries. The work of Giuliano and Narayan (2003) into travel patterns follows the common practice of using diaries that include a week's continuous activity, as does that of researchers Atkinson and Kintrea (2001) and Camina and Wood (2009), who have used activity diaries as a way of gathering data on social cohesion in gentrifying neighbourhoods. But a week is by no means the standard time span for activity and travel diaries. In research on urban mobility patterns and public transport for the working poor in Knoxville, Tennessee, Rogalsky (2010) asked respondents to complete diaries over five days. Similarly, Novak and Sykora (2007) in an ambitious study of the mobility patterns of suburbanites in the Prague metropolitan area asked diarists to produce diaries over three non-consecutive days, including one weekend day. It is important to note that the effectiveness of activity and travel diaries is dependent on the quality and clarity of the log. The instructions and coding used to fill out the log must be easy for respondents to follow, and they must – of course – gather all the parameters of detail required by the researcher. It is not possible in this chapter to provide a detailed introduction into the design and distribution of activity logs. Good overviews are provided by Jones and Stopher (2003) and Schönfelder and Axhausen (2010).

RESEARCHING THE CITY

Days(s)						What else were you doing?					
What did you do?	Start time	End time	Where did you do it?	Did anyone else do this with you?	Was anyone else around at the time?	*Please enter code and duration for up to three additional activities*					
Please write code for one main activity			*e.g. at home; at office; between home and work*	*Yes / No*	*Yes / No*	Code	Dur.	Dur.	Code	Code	Dur.

Figure 8.1 An example of an activity diary log for a diarist
Source: Kenyon (2006:126)

Communicating		Entertainment / recreation		Formal activities		Household and personal	
C1	Face to face	E1	Resting, relaxing	F1	Paid work	H1	Sleeping
C2	By telephone (landline)	E2	Reading	F2	Education	H2	Personal care
C3	By mobile telephone	E3	Do hobbies	F2I	Education – Internet	H3	Eating, drinking, inc. preparation
C4	By text, or video messaging	E4	Play sports	F3	Voluntary work	H4	Housework, household maintanance
C5	By letter	E5	Cinema, theatre, watch sport, etc.	F3I	Voluntary work – Internet	H5	Childcare
C6	By fax	E6	Social (pub, club, bingo...)	F4	Religious activity	H6	Other caring activities
C7	By email	E7	Watching TV, video, DVD	F4I	Religious activity – Internet	H7	Running errands (e.g. posting a letter)
C8	In chat room	E8	Listening to music, radio	F5	Campaigns, civic	H8	Escort (includes school run)
		E9	Travelling for pleasure	F5I	Campaigns, civic – Internet	H9	Banking, financial
		E10	Surfing (no specific purpose)			H9I	Banking, financial – Internet
		E11	Playing computer games			H10	Medical (includes GP, hospital)
CO	Other communicating	EO	Other entertainment/recreation	FO	Other formal activities	HO	Other household and personal
COI	Other communicating – Internet	EOI	Other entertainment/recreation – Internet	FOI	Other formal activities – Internet		

Information search		Shopping for		Travel		Other / Personal	
11	Trivia	51	Groceries (main)	T1	Driving the car	01	Other activities
HI	Trivia-Internet	S1I	Groceries (main) – Internet	T1I	Travelling in car as passenger	01I	Other activities – Internet
12	Window shopping	52	Groceries (top up)	T2	Travelling on bus	02	Personal activities
121	Window shopping – Internet	S2I	Groceries (top up) – Internet	T2I	Travelling by coach	02I	Personal activities – Internet
13	Journey information	53	Clothing	T3	Travelling on train		
131	Journey information – Internet	S3I	Clothing – Internet	T3I	Riding motorcycle, or similar		
14	Employment information	54	Music	T4	Travelling in taxi		
141	Employment information – Internet	S4I	Music-Internet	T4I	Riding bicycle		
15	Hobbies	55	Journeys (not holidays)	T5	Walking		
151	Hobbies-Internet	S5I	Journeys (not holidays) – Internet	T5I	Travelling on an aeroplane		
16	Medical (inc. NHS Direct)						
161	Medical – Internet						
17	News (includes TV, newspaper)						
171	News-Internet						
10	Other information search	SO	Other shopping	TO	Other travel		
101	Other information search – Internet	SOI	Other shopping – Internet				

Figure 8.2 The coding used to complete the diary

Source: Kenyon (2006:128)

Solicited written and photographic diaries

Activity and travel diaries focus on collecting sets of very tightly defined data. Other researchers employ diaries to generate more impressionistic and interpretatively oriented research material (Housel 2009; Jackson et al. 2006; Meth 2003, 2004). Like quantitatively oriented diary researchers, these researchers are interested in the rhythm and flow of people's activity through and in urban environments. However, they are also interested in the interpretative accounts that their respondents can offer about their activities through the day. Such diaries are known as solicited diaries, because while they do tend to follow the format of the kind of personal diary many people keep, they have been commissioned, or *solicited*, by the researcher. The remit of a diary can vary enormously. In some cases diarists are simply provided with a diary and asked to describe their day. In other cases, diarists are asked to focus only on certain kinds of activities, or activities that take place in particular places. A written diary may contain elements of a diary log. For example, a researcher may be interested in the everyday movements of an individual and would like to use the material from the diary to produce a map of the diarist's daily movements. In this case the researcher may instruct the diarist to include very specific details about journeys undertaken, their timing, and purpose (see Figure 8.3).

With photographic diaries – which have been used by researchers like Datta (2012), Johnsen et al. (2008) and Young and Barrett (2001) – respondents are asked to describe or illustrate elements of their life through the medium of photography. Typically respondents are given a disposable camera and asked to photograph that which the respondent feels is most relevant. The period over which they are asked to carry the diary camera can vary greatly. In Johnsen et al.'s (2008: 197) study of homeless men and women, the recruited diarists were 'simply asked to carry [the camera] with them for one week and to take pictures of the places that they utilised in daily life and/or that were in some way important to them'. In her study of east European migrants in London, Datta (2012: 1730) asked her respondents to carry a camera around for a month and take 'pictures of any aspect of living in London'. The time frame not withstanding, once the camera is full the diary is usually understood to be finished. This obviously limits the scope of the diary. However, digital cameras offer a range of possibilities for widening the remit of the diarist – as they allow the diarist to take many more photographs, as well as allowing them to delete, edit, and retake photographs that they are unhappy with. In some cases, diarists might be asked to note down when and where each individual photograph was taken, and why the photograph was taken. This is by no means universal. In most cases, upon the completion of the diary the diarist will talk through the photographs taken with the researcher. An advantage of photographic diaries is that they do not require any degree of literacy. This is useful when working with children, as Young and Barrett (2001) demonstrate in their photographic diary-based study of Kampala street children. A further advantage is that, compared to a written diary, in general, photographic diaries require a lesser time commitment. Rather than having to compose a written diary entry the diarist simply has to point a camera and take photographs. While photographic diaries represent a discrete form of diary production, in practice photographic diaries are often combined with written diaries.

The practice of interviewing diarists about the activities included in their dairies is commonplace. For researchers like Camina and Wood (2009), in-depth interviews with a number of diary respondents is used to supplement the quantitative data provided by the respondents' diary logs (see Chapter 4, this volume). However, following the lead of ethnographers Zimmerman and Wieder (1977), a number of urban researchers have made interviews that are based directly around the material in respondents' diaries central to their methodology. In Middleton's (2009, 2010) research into the practice of walking to work in north-east London, participants were asked to write diaries of their journey to work. On the completion of the diary, participants were then guided through a in-depth interview based around the material in the diary. A similar technique had earlier been used by Latham (2004, 2006) in his research into the changing public culture of parts of inner-city Auckland. In effect, in the diary interview the diarist is asked to lead the researcher through the diary. This allows the diarists to explain ambiguities in their written diary. It also provides the diarist with an opportunity to reflect upon and expand on the accounts presented in the diary. An example of a similar approach based around a contact diary log followed by a diary log interview can be found in Conradson and Latham's (2007) work on transnational migrants in London. A small number of researchers have also explored the possibility of producing video-based diaries. Video diaries can

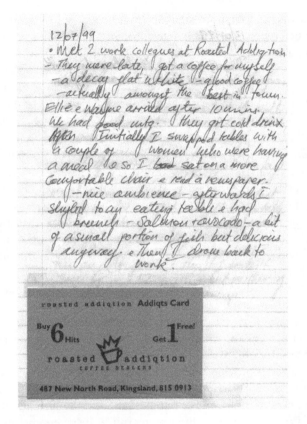

Figure 8.3 An extract from a written diary

Source: Author

be of two forms. They may involve the diarist simply talking to a static video camera, recounting the events of a day. Or the video camera might be used as a device to record key elements of a respondent's day, a child's journey to school for example. The advantage of video is that through the ability to record significant blocks of time, and in catching movement, it provides an immediacy of context difficult to match in written and photographic diaries. The usefulness of the diary is very dependent on the ability of the diarist to competently use the equipment provided for them to produce a diary.

The practicalities of organizing respondent diaries

So far the chapter has emphasized the advantages of diaries as a research tool. However, it should be stressed that organizing the collection of diary-based data is necessarily an involved, drawn out, and far-from-straightforward process. In this the method is not dissimilar to other types of research (see Chapter 2, this volume). This is the case whether talking about highly structured activity diaries or more free-form solicited diaries. That said, following a few simple rules can aid in the smooth running of a respondent diary-based research project. Readers interested in carrying out a purely quantitative activity and travel diary should perhaps skip the rest of this section and go straight to the more technical account offered in Jones and Stopher (2003).

1. *Think carefully about what kind of information you want to generate from respondent diaries.* If your main interest is obtaining accurate details about when people engage in a certain activity it may be superfluous to ask them to write about everything they do during a week. Similarly, if you are interested in the general texture of a person's day it may be inhibiting to demand that a diarist lists the exact time and date of everything recorded in the diary. In fact, it is a good idea to spend a few days, or better, a week, filling out a diary in the manner that you intend to ask your respondents to. This will allow you to think about the details you would like your diarists to focus on, and the appropriate strategies that need to be adopted to facilitate this focus.

2. *Think carefully about who you want to recruit as diarists and how you are going to recruit them.* The recruitment of diarists is often the most time-consuming part of the research process. If you are fortunate you may have an existing research contact who will be able to provide willing diarists. More commonly you will have to think creatively about how to recruit diarists. The most reliable technique is to ask acquaintances if they know people who fit the profile of the kinds of respondent diarists you are wishing to recruit. Advertisements in local or community newspapers, listing magazines such as London's *Time Out*, or notices on Internet discussion boards, can also be effective.

3. *Think about the competencies of the people you are recruiting as diarists.* One of the great strengths of solicited diaries is that they draw on the narrative skills of those producing them. This, of course, demands that if you are going to ask a certain population of people to produce a diary, they must have those skills. If you are working with a social group with a low level of literacy, written diaries may not be appropriate. Or, rather, you may be able to gain diary accounts only from relatively highly educated and privileged groups (although see Meth 2003; Thomas 2007). In this case, another form of diary keeping, such as photographic diaries, might be more appropriate.

4. *Provide diarists with a clear briefing of what you expect them to do.* Diarists need to have a good sense of what they are being asked to produce. They also need to have a reasonable sense of the purpose of the project to which they are contributing. Ideally the researcher should brief the diarist in person. This gives diarists the chance to clarify with the researcher just what they are being asked to do. Respondents should also be provided with a detailed instruction sheet. The instruction sheet should include information about who is undertaking the research, the institution the

researcher is affiliated with, and contact details for both the researcher and others involved in supervising the research project. The instruction sheet should be firmly attached to the diary that is given to the diarist to complete.

5. *Provide your diarists with a diary log or notebook (or camera if doing a photographic diary) and a pen.* As the researcher is asking people to produce a diary the researcher must provide the diary. The diary or log should be robust, easy to carry around and have enough pages for the respondent to complete the task asked of them. Obviously, respondents will also need a pen to fill out the diary.

6. *Devise a straightforward procedure for returning completed diaries.* Getting diaries back from diarists can be surprisingly time-consuming. The most reliable way of getting diaries returned is to pick them up directly from the diarist. This has the advantage that you can ask the diarist about how they found the diary writing process. If you are combining the diary with diary-interviews the diary pick-up also offers an opportunity to arrange a time for the interview. However, if you have a number of diarists writing at the same time, your diarists are very busy, or your diarists are dispersed over a large area, it may not be practicable to personally pick up each diary. In this case, you should provide diarists with a prepaid self-addressed envelope and instruct the diarist to post the completed diary.

What kinds of material might you expect? And what to do with it?

The kind of research material generated through respondent diaries is dependent on the instructions given to the respondent diarists. In the case of activity and travel diaries the diarist will have produced a set of responses that should be easily assimilated into a quantitative database. There are any number of excellent statistical and geographic information handbooks that can guide the urban researcher through this process (see for example Longley et al. 2011; Walford 2011). Material from solicited diaries should be approached like any other set of qualitative data. It is good practice to type out the text of the diary either into a word processing document or a qualitative research program such as NVivo or The Ethnograph. The quality and detail of diaries may vary enormously. This can present problems. Try not to treat shorter, less-detailed diaries simply as failures that should be ignored. It is always tempting to organize any research account primarily around diary material generated from the most loquacious and personable diarists, but this temptation should be resisted. While the longer and more detailed diaries may offer more obvious sources for quotation and illustration, the shortness of other diaries might well point to equally important conclusions. Be prepared to recognize that there are multiple realities to any social situation and work hard to construct research accounts that pay due respect to that. If you have combined the solicited diaries with interviews you should analyse these as you would with any other interview material. Once you have transcribed the interviews it is helpful to spiral-bind a copy of the original solicited diary along with copies of the transcribed diary and transcribed interview.

The limitations of research respondent-produced diaries

Diaries can yield research material that is enormously productive. However, it is important to stress the limitations of diaries as a research technique.

First, diaries make significant demands on both the researcher and – if they go beyond the single 24 hours of some activity diaries – the research respondent. For the researcher the logistics of finding appropriate diarists, of distributing the diaries, ensuring that diaries are completed in a manner that is aligned with the project's research aims, ensuring the retrieval of completed diaries, and arranging diary interviews should not be underestimated. Of course, all good research is demanding of a researcher's time and intellectual resources, so this is no different. More crucially, diaries make a much greater demand on a research respondent's time than more commonly employed techniques such as interviews or focus groups. As Cochrane discusses in Chapter 4 of this volume, interviews often last no more than an hour or two. Even research that involves follow up interviews often involves a time commitment by the respondent of no more than three to four hours. However, diaries require an on-going commitment from the diarist. This can make it difficult to recruit diarists. And it may mean that many groups who would make ideal diary subjects will refuse to write diaries owing to the time constraints they are under.

Second, as has already been mentioned, diary keeping assumes a certain set of personal competencies. Producing a diary requires certain basic skills: an ability to write, or an ability to use a camera, an ability to keep track of the passage of time and so on. It might be assumed that these skills are generally distributed in most populations. However, even in highly educated societies like those in the United Kingdom, Europe, America or Canada there are wide variations in people's levels of literacy, capacity for self-organization and so on. Even highly competent individuals may find completing a diary intimidating, especially if in their normal day-to-day life they are rarely called upon to produce self-directed blocks of handwritten text. Indeed, given the contemporary ubiquity of computer and keyboard use it may well be necessary to devise on-line forms of diary keeping as handwriting becomes for many an archaic – and thus alien – technique of communication.

Third, solicited diaries – whether written or photographic – can produce an enormous variety in the quality and depth of material generated. If one of the advantages of the diary technique is that they allow the respondent diarist to stand in for the researcher, the flip side of this is that many people are (sadly) rather poor observers and reporters.

Using GPS devices and web-based social networking as diaries

Given that producing diaries of any kind is a significant imposition on those asked to write them; given that many people are rather poor observers and reporters; and given the difficulty of generating enough diary material to construct reliable accounts, some researchers have sought to employ technological proxies for diaries. For those interested in collecting quantitative data about people's movement through cities, global positioning systems (GPS) devices are potentially revolutionary. GPS technologies are becoming ubiquitous in many devices and they offer a cheap and uniquely detailed avenue for gathering information about people's activities in cities. Mackett et al. (2007), for example, have used GPS tracking devices along with accelerometers to map school children's journeys to and from school. This technique produced a wealth of information about the differences between the actions and energy expenditures of children accompanied by adults and those unattended, between girls and boys, and between the journey to school (which tends to be very direct) and that from school in the afternoon (which tends to be slower and more meandering, especially when unaccompanied).

Social media technologies such as Twitter and online blogs have also been seen as a potentially rich form of data. Twitter posts can be treated as forms of virtual micro-diaries; they might, for example, reveal information about the rhythms and variations in mood across the day, week, or even year. The sociologists Golder and Macy (2011) gathered data from over 300 million tweets and used the material to produce 'mood maps' of America. Whilst some of the more general results from such research might appear somewhat obvious – Americans tend to get up 2 hours later on Sundays, and are more cheerful in the morning – what is really interesting about such material is the micro-variations they reveal. Indeed, some researchers, such as Peter Dodds and colleagues (2011), have argued that the real-time monitoring of social media might soon become as important a metric of societal well-being as conventional indicators like unemployment rates or GDP.

Conclusion

This chapter has provided an introduction to the use of respondent diaries.

- Urban researchers have used diaries in a number of different ways to generate material about the rhythms and routines of people's day-to-day lives.
- Activity and travel diaries are highly prescriptive and oriented towards generated data for quantitative analysis.
- Solicited written and photographic diaries tend to focus on the production of more impressionistic and interpretative accounts. The content of solicited diaries may be highly prescriptive, or left entirely up to the prerogatives of the diarist.
- Organizing a diary-based research project is an involved and sometimes complicated process. The researcher must provide clear guidelines about how they want

diarists to approach their diaries. The researcher must also provide a concise sense of the purpose of the research the diary is being solicited for.

- Diaries are often used in close conjunction with other methods such as interviews, surveys, or participant observation.
- An in-depth interview based around a completed diary can often provide an excellent supplement to a written or photographic diary.
- Research material generated through diary-based techniques can be analysed in a range of ways using standard social scientific analytic techniques.
- Some researchers have begun exploring the possibility of using GPS devices and social media technologies as ways to generate what are essentially electronic diaries of peoples' everyday activities and routines.

Frequently Asked Questions

1. When should I think about using diaries as part of a research project?

Urban researchers have used diaries as they offer a focused, structured method through which to gather data about people's routines. If a research project centres on the routines and rhythms of a particular population or group, diaries are a good tool through which to gather research material.

2. What kinds of diaries have urban researchers used?

Urban researchers have used a wide range of different diary formats. Quantitative researchers have used rigidly structured activity diaries. More qualitatively oriented researchers have used solicited diaries that give respondents latitude about what to include in a diary. Photographic diaries have also become popular. The kind of diary you should use for your own project depends on the overall aims of your research.

3. Can diaries be used as a stand-alone research method?

Yes. Many researchers have used diaries as their principal data-gathering method. It is, however, common to find diaries being used in conjunction with other methods, such as interviews.

4. What is the main drawback of using diaries as an urban research tool?

Producing diaries is necessarily time-consuming for both the researcher and the research respondent.

Follow Up References

Alaszewski, A. (2006) *Using Diaries for Social Research*. London: Sage.

This offers a comprehensive overview of the many ways diaries have been used in the social sciences.

Axhausen, K.W., Zimmermann, A., Schönfelder, S., Rindsfüser, G. and Haupt, T. (2002) Observing the rhythms of daily life: a six-week travel diary. *Transportation*, 29: 95–124.

This provides an interesting example of an extended travel-diary-based study.

Jones, P. and Stopher, P. (2003) *Transport Survey Quality and Innovation*. Oxford: Pergamon Press.

This provides an accessible and comprehensive guide to using activity and travel diaries. It includes examples of diary logs and a neat summary of the history of the use of such diaries.

Mackett, J., Gong, Y., Kitazawa, K. and Paskins, J. (2007) *Setting Children Free: Children's Independent Movement in the Local Environment* (CASA Working Paper Series). London: Centre for Advanced Spatial Analysis.

This provides a fantastic example of the potential of GPS tracking.

Meth, P. (2004) Using diaries to understand women's responses to crime and violence. *Environment and Urbanization*, 16: 153–64.

This reflection on the advantages of using respondent diaries provides a compelling example of the capacity of diaries to generate research material about emotionally sensitive issues.

Middleton, J. (2009) Stepping in time: walking, time, and space in the city. *Environment and Planning A*, 41: 1943–61.

This is a thought-provoking study of the practice of walking to work in London using solicited written and photographic diaries; it demonstrates the usefulness of diaries for conveying a sense both of the texture of an experience, and how that experience is related to wider routines.

Neuhaus, F. (ed.) (2011) *Studies in Temporal Urbanism: The Urban Tick Experiment*. London: Springer.

This provides an interesting if eclectic collection of work on urban rhythms and diaries.

References

Appold, S. and Yuen, B. (2007) Families in flats, revisited. *Urban Studies*, 44: 569–89.

Atkinson, R. and Kintrea, K. (2001) Disentangling area effects: evidence from deprived and non-deprived neighbourhoods. *Urban Studies*, 38: 2277–98.

Axhausen, K.W., Zimmermann, A., Schönfelder, S., Rindsfüser, G. and Haupt, T. (2002) Observing the rhythms of daily life: a six-week travel diary. *Transportation*, 29: 95–124.

Becker, H.S. (2007) *Telling About Society*. Chicago: University of Chicago Press.

Boarnet, M., Joh, K., Siembab, W., Fulton, W. and Nguyen, M. (2011) Retrofitting the suburbs to increase walking: evidence from a land-use-travel study. *Urban Studies*, 48: 129–59.

Brown, A., Khattak, A. and Rodriguez, D. (2008) Urban studies, neighbourhood types, travel and body mass: a study of new urbanist and suburban neighbourhoods in the US. *Urban Studies*, 45: 963–88.

Camina, M. and Wood, M. (2009) Parallel lives: towards a greater understanding of what mixed communities can offer. *Urban Studies*, 46: 459–80.

Cirillo, C. and Axhausen, K.W. (2006) Evidence on the distribution of values of travel time savings from a six-week diary. *Transportation Research Part A*, 40: 444–57.

Conradson, D. and Latham, A. (2007) The affectual possibilities of London: Antipodean transnationals and the overseas experience. *Mobilities*, 2: 231–54.

Datta, A. (2012) 'Where is the global city?' Visual narratives of London among East European migrants. *Urban Studies*, 49: 1725–40.

Dodds, P., Harris, K., Kloumann, I., Bliss, C. and Danforth, C. (2011) Temporal patterns of happiness and information in a global social network: hedonometrics and Twitter. *PLOS ONE*, 6 (12): e26752. doi:10.1371/journal.pone.0026752.

Fan, Y., Khattak, A. and Rodriguez, D. (2011) Household excess travel and neighbourhood characteristics: associations and trade-offs. *Urban Studies*, 48: 1235–53.

Giuliano, G. and Narayan, D. (2003) Another look at travel patterns and urban form: the US and Great Britain. *Urban Studies*, 40: 2295–312.

Golder, S. and Macy, M. (2011) Diurnal and seasonal mood vary with work, sleep and daylength across diverse cultures. *Science*, 30 September.

Housel, J. (2009) Geographies of whiteness: the active construction of racialized privilege in Buffalo, New York. *Social and Cultural Geography*, 10: 131–51.

Jackson, P., del Aguila, R., Clarke, I., Hallsworth, A., de Kervenoael, R. and Kirkup, M. (2006) Retail restructuring and consumer choice 2. Understanding consumer choice at the household level. *Environment and Planning A*, 38: 47–67.

Johnsen, S., May, J. and Cloke, P. (2008) Imag(in)ing 'homeless places': using auto-photography to (re)examine the geographies of homelessness. *Area*, 40: 194–207.

Jones, P. and Stopher, P. (2003) *Transport Survey Quality and Innovation*. Oxford: Pergamon Press.

Kenyon, S. (2006) The 'accessibility diary': discussing a new methodological approach to understand the impact of Internet use upon personal travel and activity participation. *Journal of Transport Geography*, 14: 123–34.

Latham, A. (2004) Researching and writing everyday accounts of the city: an introduction to the diary–photo diary–interview method, in C. Knowles and P. Sweetman (eds), *Picturing the Social Landscape: Visual Methods and the Sociological Imagination*. London: Routledge, pp. 117–31.

Latham, A. (2006) Sociality and the cosmopolitan imagination: national, cosmopolitan and local imaginaries in Auckland, New Zealand, in J. Binny, J. Holloway, S. Millington and C. Young (eds), *Cosmopolitan Urbanism*. London: Routledge, pp. 89–111.

Laurier, E. and Philo, C. (2003) The region in the boot: mobilising lone subjects and multiple objects. *Environment and Planning D*, 21: 85–106.

Lefebvre, H. (2004) *Rhythmanalysis: Space, Time and Everyday Life*. London: Continuum.

Longley, P., Goodchild, M., Maguire, D. and Rhind, D. (2011) *Geographical Information Systems and Science* (3rd edn). Hoboken, NJ: John Wiley.

Mackett, J., Gong, Y., Kitazawa, K. and Paskins, J. (2007) *Setting Children Free: Children's Independent Movement in the Local Environment* (CASA Working Paper Series). London: Centre for Advanced Spatial Analysis.

Meth, P. (2003) Entries and omissions: using solicited diaries in geographical research. *Area*, 35(2): 195–205.

Meth, P. (2004) Using diaries to understand women's responses to crime and violence. *Environment and Urbanization*, 16: 153–64.

Middleton, J. (2009) Stepping in time: walking, time, and space in the city. *Environment and Planning A*, 41: 1943–61.

Middleton, J. (2010) Sense and the city: exploring the embodied geographies of urban walking. *Social and Cultural Geography*, 11: 575–96.

Neuhaus, F. (ed.) (2011) *Studies in Temporal Urbanism: The Urban Tick Experiment*. London: Springer.

Novák, J. and Sýkora, L. (2007) A city in motion: time–space activity and mobility patterns of suburban inhabitants and the structuration of the spatial organization of the Prague metropolitan area. *Geografiska Annaler: Series B, Human Geography*, 89 (2): 147–68.

Rogalsky, J. (2010) The working poor and what GIS reveals about the possibilities of public transit. *Journal of Transport Geography*, 18: 226–37.

Schönfelder, S. and Axhausen, K.W. (2010) *Urban Rhythms and Travel Behaviour: Spatial and Temporal Phenomena of Daily Travel*. Farnham: Ashgate.

Thomas, F. (2007) Eliciting emotions in HIV/AIDS research: a diary-based ap-proach. *Area*, 39 (1): 74–82.

Valentine, G. (1999) A corporeal geography of consumption. *Environment and Planning D: Society and Space*, 17: 329–51.

Walford, N. (2011) *Practical Statistics for Geographers and Earth Scientists*. Oxford: Wiley Blackwell.

Young, L. and Barrett, H. (2001) Adapting visual methods: action research with Kampala street children. *Area*, 33: 141–52.

Zimmerman, D. and Wieder, D. (1977) The diary: diary interview method. *Urban Life*, 5: 479–98.

USING DIARIES TO STUDY URBAN WORLDS

9

GIS: A METHOD AND PRACTICE

Matthew W. Wilson

Introduction

Geographic information systems (GIS) not only provide the means to study the city, in the traditional sense of gathering and analyzing data about the city, but more broadly, enable urban researchers to enact multiple modes of inquiry – ethnographic, quantitative, qualitative, critical, historical, and the more-than-representational (see Kwan 2007). The use of the acronym 'GIS' may refer to a specific software package or to a whole suite of visual technologies used to represent the Earth. The technology may stupefy your audience or excite them with visions of a finally realized Digital Earth. It may cause other colleagues to raise an eyebrow ('Is positivism alive and well?') or to congratulate you on doing something 'practical' or 'applied' ('You're making the discipline relevant!'). Perhaps no other 'method' within geography would incite such varied responses, and yet, for many in and outside academe, GIS is *the* method produced by the geographical tradition. However, GIS is not just a tool, not just a software package. Rather, it motivates a method; it implies an inquiry and a perspective, a way to view and to represent. Consideration of the use of GIS should motivate a methodology, that is, a study of the implications/affordances of such a method. As you begin your dissertation, this chapter will assist you in understanding the issues raised by your use of GIS.

In this chapter I trace the various ways in which GIS may be used to research the city, providing some examples from my own work and that of others to discuss the appropriateness of GIS as a method, while providing the basics for examining GIS as a practice. In your dissertation on the city, GIS may simply be a way to produce representations of your research results. For other types of dissertations, GIS will be used to conduct analyses of spatial phenomena. GIS may also be used as a prompt or an illustration used to engage research subjects. In research I conducted on the use of spatial technologies to map community quality-of-life, GIS served as both the prompt in qualitative research with community members, and as a vehicle for analyzing and visualizing the data created by community members (see Wilson 2011a).

Throughout this chapter I'll be making reference to a single map produced during my research in Seattle. This research examined the use of mobile devices by a Seattle-based nonprofit in mapping quality-of-life concerns. Figure 9.1 depicts the ten neighborhoods that participated in this survey project from 2004 to 2007. The graduated circles on each neighborhood were produced by GIS to visually analyze the differences between the total features coded in each neighborhood. Through typical steps of GIS use (data collection, preparation, analysis, and visualization), this map was not only used to address the central research question of the project (that is, how neighborhoods participated in the production of digital spatial data), but was also enrolled in discussions with community members and nonprofit staff that participated in the four years of surveying. The map shows what seems to be greater participation in the Greenwood Phinney Ridge and the International District neighborhoods, and begs two questions: Why were more features coded and who participated in the survey activity?

Maps and GIS are objects that evoke and provoke. They do work beyond the desktop of the analyst, and urban researchers are well placed for examining this work. I will use Figure 9.1 to illustrate my discussion of GIS as method and practice. This chapter is organized into five sections. Following a basic introduction of GIS as a method and practice, the second section outlines necessary preparation when engaging in the use of GIS for urban research, focusing particularly on conceptualization and formalization. In the third section, I discuss observation and analysis as the *doing* of GIS-based research. The writing up of this research, its representation, is presented in section four, followed by a concluding section that outlines the affordances and limitations of the GIS method.

Introducing GIS

Those working with GIS may reference 'GIScience' as the field in which scholarship about or with GIS takes place. GIScience is a relatively recent invention, with a contested history (Schuurman 2000). Before beginning your dissertation, you should

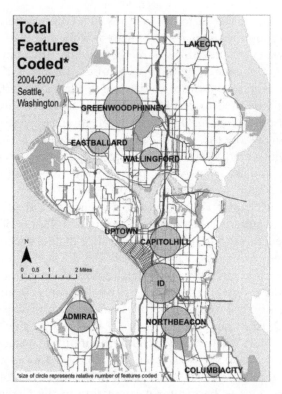

Figure 9.1   Map of Seattle neighborhoods participating in community quality-of-life surveying

take some time to consider how this history impacts GIS as a method and practice. Early in the 1990s, geographers were debating what role GIS should play in the discipline (Clark 1992; Macgill 1990). Some felt that GIS might aid a discipline that was seen to be increasingly disparate in intellectual interests, that the technology would provide the glue to bind together modes of geographical inquiries (Dobson 1993; Openshaw 1991, 1992). Others were less optimistic – even antagonistic – and felt GIS was weakening the discipline, reducing the tradition to the accumulation of 'facts', as well as linking geography to projects of violence and domination (Lake 1993; Pickles 1993; Smith 1992; Taylor 1990; Taylor and Overton 1991). Through a series of interventions, an initiative labeled 'GIS and Society' sought to address this chasm by generating a multipart research agenda, eventually leading to the development of subfields like participatory and public participation GIS, spatial decision support systems and collaborative GIS, critical, feminist and qualitative GIS, and the spatial humanities (for overviews and edited collections towards this end, see Bodenhamer et al. 2010; Cope and Elwood 2009; Craig et al. 2002; Dragicevic and Balram 2006; Pickles 1995, 2006; Sheppard 1995, 2005). The application of GIS to urban research stems from these various subfields, each of which mark a multiplicity of approaches, methodological challenges, and forms of public engagement.

Furthermore, a chapter on the use of GIS in researching the city would be neglect-ful if it did not briefly mention the myriad ways in which GIS is central to the city – its planning, management, destruction, reinvention, as well as to those that hope to profit within its borders. Reflect on the ways in which GIS impacts your everyday life. Geospatial technologies represent a multi-billion dollar global industry, and impact everyday urban experiences, embedded in consumer electronics and throughout the military–industrial complex to route goods/services/consumers and direct predator drones and 'smart' bombs. They have become so central to daily life in advanced capitalist societies as to become invisible, part of our technological unconscious (Thrift 2004). Spatialized codes direct how we search the Internet (Zook and Graham 2007), how we use air travel (Budd and Adey 2009), how we track urban quality-of-life (Wilson 2011b), and how we interact in the living rooms of our homes (Dodge and Kitchin 2009). Regardless of our awareness, systems for geographic information underline our being in the urban. More explicitly, GIS has been used in a variety of urban functions: in community and urban planning (Elwood 2002; Talen 2000), as well as transportation planning (Nyerges and Aguirre 2011), in public service delivery (Longley 2005), and in disaster response (Zook et al. 2010).

As a result, using GIS to study the city may mean using one or more technologies. You might be using GPS (global positioning systems), which could mean con-sumer-grade handheld receivers or survey-grade receivers (distinguished by their levels of positional accuracy and attributal sophistication). Or it could indicate that you are using GPS trackers (that might clip on to a human or other object of study) or the (assisted) GPS application on many mobile phones. You might also be using for-profit desktop software suites like Esri's ArcGIS or Google Earth, or open-source software like GRASS or QGIS. You might have heard about web-based GIS and map mashups, created using tools like Google MyMaps, Esri's ArcGIS Online, or OpenStreetMap. You might have heard about something called 'qualitative GIS', and wonder where you might download such software (you can't ... yet). Depending on where you are completing your studies, you may not have ready access to some technologies. Start by consulting with your institution's GIS instructor, or if there is no one, check the technology offerings at your library. This would not be the most appropriate venue for cataloging all the systems, platforms, and software tools avail-able (there are no doubt Wikipedia entries that serve this purpose). However, think-ing of GIS as a 'method' exposes some preliminary questions and concerns that this chapter will now discuss: How do you express your understanding of the world in the computational structures of GIS? What are the specific considerations for spatial datasets? How do you represent the results of your work with GIS?

Preparing for research

GIS is used in multiple ways to research the city. As such, there can be no single 'step-by-step' process that works across all cases. Pavlovskaya (2004) uses GIS to understand the economics of everyday life in Moscow. Brown and Knopp (2008) use GIS in their study of queer oral histories in Seattle. Kwan (2008) uses GIS to visualize emotional geographies in Columbus, Ohio. Elwood (2006) works with community partners to use GIS in neighborhood organizing and planning. In each project, GIS is used in different ways in the process of preparing for and doing research. As you prepare to do your dissertation using GIS, you will need to engage in the interrelated processes of conceptualization and formalization, understood as:

1. Considering the role of the map/GIS/data in research.
2. Formalizing both the elements to be included within GIS as well as the practices with GIS.

Both conceptualization and formalization are important stages in GIS research. Even projects that may not seem to explicitly engage in conceptualization and formalization nonetheless must assume certain relationships between the objects represented by data and their material, physical manifestations: 'reality'. Fundamentally, these relationships are engaged through explicit discussions of the practices of conceptualization and formalization.

Conceptualization

It is helpful to begin with Nadine Schuurman's (2006: 730) thoughts on the important disjunctures between conceptualization and formalization. In her research on GIS ontologies (understood simply as the categories that compose data), she writes:

> If we think of conceptualization as a cognate step toward understanding spatial processes and relationships, there remains a pressing need to express those relationships in a mathematical or formal notation as a precursor to coding them.

Conceptualization in GIS research is a process by which a researcher not only makes sense of spatiality, but, to extend Schuurman, must also consider the relationships between the mapping technologies, the focus of the map, and the audience that views the map. In this sense, conceptualization is asking: What role does the map/GIS play in research?

- as prompt/illustration for inquiry (e.g. a map used in a focus group discussion about neighborhood improvements)
- as vehicle for analysis (e.g. a GIS to compute the travel times of suburban residents)
- as participative/collaborative object (e.g. a map made through the deliberations of community members to define a neighborhood boundary dispute) or

- as a system for building visualizations (e.g. a GIS to model views from high points in the city).

The asking of this question underlines the entanglements of epistemology and method. Here it is useful to recall the arguments around quantitative geography in the 1990s (Lawson 1995), more recently reinvigorated by qualitative GIS (Pavlovskaya 2009): namely that methods need not presume or assume a singular way of knowing. Certainly, particular ways of knowing are enabled or made easier with the use of particular methods, but this need not be an automatic relationship. This is not to say that methods are, or can be, neutrally applied. Instead, it is an insistence on the creative role of the method – one that adapts and enrolls the epistemological stance of the researcher (see Chapter 2, this volume).

Conceptualization and formalization demands attention to the entire research process, as part of your preparations. Figure 9.2 sketches an ordering of different aspects of research, beginning with conceptualization and formalization. During research preparation it becomes important to consider the inputs/outputs of each aspect of research, as is true of many research endeavors. What is it that research is producing, at each stage? How will GIS be used? What are the requirements for these productions?

conceptualization → formalization → observation → analysis → representation

Figure 9.2 Ordered aspects of research. GIS may intervene at any or all aspects of research

While these various stages of research are each important to consider as you prepare to use GIS, thinking about the analysis stage may be fruitful for understanding how to prepare. Despite common notions of GIS as a tool for spatial analysis, GIS need not be understood only as the chief vehicle for analysis in your study, and its use may actually precede analysis. Nor does GIS necessarily have to be used only for the representation of results from the analysis.

Figure 9.3 presents these three relationships of GIS to the analysis stage of urban research in Figure 9.2. In conceptualizing where GIS is used in the process of research, you will be better able to outline the entire project. By preceding analysis (relationship 'A'), GIS might be used as a prompt in an ethnographic project to engage research participants in a discussion of an urban issue (perceptions of crime, effects of gentrification, historical preservation, etc.). The GIS acts as an illustration in a data collection effort, prior to analysis. GIS acting as the vehicle for analysis (relationship 'B') is perhaps the most prevalent assumption about the role of GIS in research (that a researcher collects data, feeds them into a GIS, and results appear!). Another prevalent assumption is that GIS are used as a final stage in the research process, following analysis (relationship 'C'), to create maps of the results of the study. In planning your dissertation you need to think long and hard about how you intend to use GIS.

```
(A)  GIS precedes analysis

(B)  GIS is the analysis

(C)  GIS follows analysis
```

Figure 9.3 Relationship of analysis to GIS

Formalization

Moving from conceptualization to formalization is the subject of much consternation in GIScience, particularly for those approaching the use of GIS from a critical human geography perspective, as many of the concepts of critical urban research may not be reduced to the computational vision of GIS (Schuurman 2006). In other words, as you prepare to do research, you may discover that the formalizations necessary for a particular line of inquiry are beyond the capacities of GIS. For instance, much of critical urban research may explicitly reject the grid epistemology associated with GIS. In post-structural research, for example, there is an assumption that the categories of the study evolve over its duration (see Dixon and Jones 1998). However, to use GIS is to make formal arrangements: What scale is utilized in your urban research? How is the city to be represented on the map? What spatial phenomena can be expressed in Euclidean space?

Once a researcher begins to formalize their conceptualizations central to their project, the affordances and limitations of GIS as method and practice will become apparent. There are a seemingly endless number of formal and formative factors to consider at this stage of the process, categorized here as:

1. data constraints
2. method constraints, and
3. system constraints.

Of course, how a researcher makes decisions about these factors is directly dependent upon the relationship of GIS to analysis (see Figure 9.3). Therefore, 'data' may mean something different where GIS is used prior to analysis, compared to more ethnographic projects, where the GIS may operate as a prompt in discussions with research participants. 'Data', in an ethnographic project, may take the form of field notes and interview transcripts (see Chapter 5, this volume).

However, regardless of the relationship of GIS to analysis, a researcher needs digital data for GIS work. Prior to 'doing research' then, the researcher needs to consider how certain variables in the research project (race, class, gender, sexuality, property, home, public space, etc.) will be incorporated into the GIS and operationalized. As part of the process of formalization, operationalization entails making decisions about how to measure the variables selected by the researcher. For instance, a dissertation interested in the spatiality of class in an urban area might consider using income measures from a national census as one indicator of 'class'. Such data are constrained by the spatial geometry of the enumeration areas, without which the operationalization of 'class' using the spatial analytical capabilities of GIS would not be possible.

As you prepare to conduct work with GIS, consider how the method addresses the research question. It is tempting at the formalization stage to reconfigure the research question such that the available technical capability of the GIS can directly be enrolled. If the method available within GIS constrains the research question 'too much', perhaps the method is inappropriate. Relatedly, GIS are computer-based systems that have their own constraints – maximum data sizes, bandwidth restrictions, physical memory limitations, etc. – each of which may make the research question and the selected method untenable. These constraints are important to consider as a researcher prepares to conduct a study using these systems. Put directly, GIS are software with real limits.

Furthermore, not all data and methods are equally appropriate, and researchers will need to consider how different kinds of data were created and manipulated as they formalize their project. Metadata is an important way of getting at appropriateness and is, very simply, data about data. GIS research relies upon metadata to understand basic issues of projection and accuracy as well as more database-level concerns about attribute parameters and construction. If well maintained, metadata provides a written record of the construction of spatial data as well as the manipulation of such data. Some metadata is created through standards maintained by national bodies, such as the Federal Geographic Data Committee (FGDC), while many datasets may lack properly maintained metadata. As researchers prepare to use GIS, they may need to consult with those in charge of it to better understand how the data came to be. For instance, spatial data may only be intended for particular scales, where levels of accuracy are most appropriate. Metadata may assist you in understanding whether or not particular data are appropriate for your research question.

As I prepared to create the map in Figure 9.1, I quickly realized the importance of understanding two key factors: (1) how the data categories were created and (2) how surveyors were instructed to collect information about urban quality-of-life. By speaking with those who created the software used in the survey and those who created the data categories, I better understood how the data were collected, toward what ends, which meant that my project extended from the GIS and the map to many discussions with those involved in its production. Spatial data and maps have implications beyond the often narrow ways in which they are imagined. By addressing these two factors, the project evolved into an examination of the ways in which residents were trained to see their neighborhoods as specific data objects (Wilson 2011a) as well as how the data generated by the surveys were significant in different ways to different people and organizations (Wilson 2011b).

As with many methods, the distinction between preparing for and conducting research is an artificial one. Conceptualization and formalization are integral aspects of the 'doing' of research. By enabling such separations, research runs the risk of bracketing assumptions from the research process, fixing them as neutral conditions for data collection, observations, and analyses. Instead, urban researchers that use GIS should understand the processes of conceptualization and formalization as significant, contingent stages that make the research possible. They are therefore stages to be returned to throughout the research, to re-evaluate appropriateness and perhaps adjust parameters to better address the research question (see Chapter 2, this volume). This particular way of thinking the 'doing' of GIS draws particularly upon qualitative GIS, as simultaneously both method and practice.

Doing research

Traditionally, the doing of research with GIS incorporates two aspects of research (see Figure 9.2) – observation and analysis. One must make observations and analyze such observations. Observations are dependent upon what can be measured, decisions that are made as part of the formalization stage, previously discussed. In what follows, I discuss different types of observations and related considerations. I then review a range of analytical approaches with GIS.

Observation

Broadly speaking, when *doing* GIS research you will be making observations. Depending on how a researcher views Figure 9.3 (for instance, if GIS is used as a vehicle for analysis), this section might also be titled 'data collection'. Data collection can be the most time-intensive aspect of GIS research. The lack of appropriate data can sink a research project that uses GIS, and data availability is commonly expressed as a major limitation for GIS-based research.

When locating data, there are three approaches to help guide the researcher. First, the required geographic area and scale should direct the data search (is this state or provincial data? metropolitan data? federal data?). Second, the theme of the data should help isolate organizations that might collect and maintain such data (census, housing, natural resources, urban infrastructure, transportation, etc.). Finally, by contacting individuals or organizations with interests related to the research question, the sharing of datasets may be appropriate. More specifically, there are several questions to consider when selecting GIS data:

- Are the data in a format that can be used directly in GIS (i.e. shapefile, geodatabase, kml)? If not, can the data be transformed into spatial data? Data tables that have fields like latitude and longitude or street address or administrative boundary may still be transformed into GIS data.
- Are the spatial files' coordinate system parameters defined? In order to conduct spatial analysis, the appropriate projection needs to be defined.

- What is the scale of the spatial data? Does it meet the needs of the research question? If the study is focused at the neighborhood scale, datasets like sidewalks, building footprints, and green spaces might be appropriate.
- At what summary level are the tabular data (by address, county, tract, postal code, state, etc.)? This will inform the kinds of spatial analysis that can be performed.
- How recent are the data? When were the data created and most recently updated? The currency of a dataset may directly impact the ability to ask certain research questions.
- What were the sources of the data? Data collected by governments may have specific timelines for when the data are updated.
- What are the copyright requirements? Are there distribution restrictions or human-subjects research guidelines? Some datasets may require the researcher to enter into privacy agreements, and may not be legally distributed or published.

(Adapted from Stanford University Libraries 2006)

As the researcher assembles data for analysis, these questions should help determine the appropriateness of the data for addressing the research question.

In addition to acquiring existing spatial data, or tabular data with a spatial attribute, a researcher may also need to collect additional data in the field. This might be done through GPS, using handheld receivers that record data points and lines (see Chapter 8, this volume). Many of these devices have the capability of downloading spatial data directly into a standard format ready for GIS. In contemporary urban research, data observations may also be made using street addresses, which can be stored in a spreadsheet and then be geocoded directly into the GIS.

Other types of observations with GIS may be made. If GIS are used as a discussion prompt with research participants (relationship 'A' in Figure 9.3), then 'observations' are likely ethnographic or qualitative. By working directly with research participants in using GIS, a researcher can better understand how spatial knowledge is constructed and made to do work in the city. As such, GIS may be used directly in participatory action research (Elwood 2009) to evaluate or interpret the information products created by GIS or to interrogate the categories enrolled in the process of observation itself.

Analysis

Just as the modes of observation depend upon how you formulate the role of GIS in your work, analysis is equally diverse in approach. By disentangling method from epistemology, it is possible to imagine how GIS might be used in interpretative as well as positivist modes of inquiry (Pavlovskaya 2009). Whether understood as basic measurement, calculation, modeling, or as comparative, thematization, affective, analysis is the aspect of research through which new knowledge is generated.

Chrisman (2002) organizes analytical operations with GIS from basic attributal operations (queries, categorical manipulations, and arithmetic procedures) to more

Table 9.1 Some common analytical operations used with GIS and their descriptions

Analytical operation	Description
Queries	Retrieval from an attribute database based on characteristics of a data record (may be spatial characteristics)
Categorical manipulations	Reclassifying attribute data into new categories
Arithmetic procedures	Addition, subtraction, multiplication, and division between attribute fields and between records in an attribute database
Overlays	Examines how spatial phenomena are related, such as union (all features in both input data layers) and intersection (only those features in common in both input data layers)
Buffers	Examines the proximity between features
Least-cost path	Computes the path of least resistance (time, effort, cost, etc.) between two geographic points

advanced spatial analysis (overlays, buffers, surfaces, viewsheds, and networks; see Table 9.1 and refer to any of the more popular textbooks on the use of GIS for spatial analysis). Within GIS, these operations are often organized by spatial data model: raster or vector. Vector data are composed of points, lines and polygons that use geographic coordinates as vertices. Raster data are composed of grids that store geographic information cell-by-cell, where each cell corresponds to an area on the surface of the Earth. Due to the differences in the architecture of these spatial data models (as well as the differences in their philosophies, see Couclelis 1992), certain analytical operations are connected to specific data models. For instance, networks are most efficiently analyzed using vector data, while surfaces are often represented and analyzed using raster data.

These modes of 'spatial analysis' lend themselves toward the computational, and certainly toward more quantitative data. Within the fields of qualitative GIS and the spatial humanities, scholars are exploring different modes of analysis that allow more interpretative moves within GIS and, thereby, qualitative data. The subfield of qualitative GIS is focused on the use of a mix of data types, quantitative and qualitative (Cope and Elwood 2009). As a method, qualitative GIS builds reflexivity directly into the technical operation (see Jung 2009; Knigge and Cope 2006). The growing field of spatial humanities is similarly concerned with enrolling spatial techniques in humanistic inquiry (Bodenhamer et al. 2010). The spatial humanities thus envision working with the historical and the artifactual in GIS to bridge multiple ways of knowing (see Cooper and Gregory 2011; Yuan 2010).

Within more participatory uses of GIS, qualitative research methods like discourse analysis or grounded theory may be used (see Knigge and Cope 2006; Wilson 2009). Here, the emphasis is on analyzing the GIS as a practice, as integrally part of the way the world is understood and experienced and not as a neutral bystander. For instance, the map produced in Figure 9.1 uses basic arithmetic to produce the graduated circles that represent the total number of records collected by neighborhood residents.

The GIS was used to analyze and represent the differences in the total number of records that residents collected. However, more important to this particular urban research project, the map produced in Figure 9.1 evocatively prompted residents to further discuss the significance of the differences across Seattle neighborhoods – a discussion that was analyzed using discourse analysis. Here, it is important to recognize GIS as part of, and not separate from, that discourse analysis; the technical production of knowledge intervenes directly in the more interpretative/discursive practice of making meaning.

Writing up research

After *doing* scholarly work (by means of GIS or otherwise), you will typically need to engage in a process of 'writing up' (see Chapter 11, this volume). For your dissertation, the write-up phase may be limited to your institutional adviser/supervisor, although you may want to consider circulating your results more broadly, in your portfolio or on your blog. Practically speaking, the actual writing up of GIS research is an exercise in metadata construction. As discussed earlier, metadata is a written record of the creation and manipulation of data. By writing up research, you are extending the written record of spatial data, in ways that will assist future scholars in evaluating the research as well as continuing the study. When conducting GIS work, the write up involves more than just writing a final dissertation, and includes: authoring or updating the accompanying metadata for the datasets produced by the project, making the datasets accessible to the broader public or to the specific communities affected by such data collection, as well as creating representations of the results – often in cartographic form. In this section, I discuss these three considerations as part of 'representation', the last aspect of research depicted in Figure 9.2.

Representation

As symbols that constitute reality, representations here are understood as maps or as data themselves. In the process of writing up, researchers engage in the production of these representations, producing maps for publication, documenting the representations in the form of metadata, or presenting findings to the research community or to the community impacted by such research. Due to the ways in which GIS data and maps evoke authority on a subject (King 1996; Wood 1992), the practice of representing with/through geographic information technologies demands considerable attention. These representations may travel, in that they may be enrolled into new knowledge projects (complementary or otherwise). Representation, thus, acts in excess of the agenda of the researcher. In other words, your student projects may be taken up at some point by other researchers.

As you complete your GIS projects you may be requested to share their spatial data with others conducting work on similar urban issues. Therefore, it is important to carefully document data, including information about the time period, contact information, data quality, spatial reference, attributes contained, and any additional information about how the data were collected or derived and manipulated. The practice of recording metadata allows the transfer of not just the data, but the contexts around which the data exist. This information proves of critical importance as urban researchers share and enroll others' data, to better understand the limitations or constraints around their use. In your dissertations, you may well be asked to provide a 'methods' section where you would discuss these details.

Cartographic representations are perhaps the most obvious result of GIS-based research of the city. And while maps make take several forms (web-based, paper, mobile-device ready, etc.), there are general practices of map-making that should act as guides. Consider the audience, purpose, reproduction constraints (color, black and white, digital, paper, etc.), and necessary annotations. Will there need to be a legend, a north arrow, a scale bar in your project? How will you indicate the source of the data, or the various participants in the project? Are there other visualizations that might aid the map? Yau (2011) covers a range of visualization techniques (many of which are entirely web-based) for both spatial (and non-spatial) data. The map is not decoration and should directly aid your reader in understanding the results of your project.

The map in Figure 9.1 was produced to engage Seattle residents as to the differences between the raw amount of data collected in their neighborhoods. As but one symbol of the reality of this survey effort, this representation enabled residents to further discuss their experiences with the survey, becoming an entry into more detailed discussions of residents' hopes for how these data were to be used and their concerns for how these kinds of data collections tend to justify specific urban policies. The 'writing up' of GIS work should involve such discussions of the work that representations do – by releasing the cartographic products back to the communities impacted by such representations.

Conclusion

Geographic information systems enable different ways of knowing and cannot be limited to a single method. GIS are both something one does, participates in, as well as something one uses. As media, GIS are both practice and method. In this chapter, I have described a range of concerns in both doing GIS and paying attention to how GIS practices permeate urban society. Ultimately, GIS are technologies of representation. That maps are made, as a human endeavor, complicates and haunts cartography as science, exposing the subjectivity and selective interests of cartographic practice. And while these crises of representation should not justify a dismissal of GIS, they should inspire careful consideration of the limitations and affordances of GIS as a method of researching the city.

That maps wield power is not lost on critical cartographers. As representations of space, maps produce territories. Maps, and the GIS that create them, insinuate themselves into everyday life, figuring our interactions with human and nonhuman others. They communicate expertise and authenticity, where none may exist. Maps may challenge the status quo or reinforce it. As Harris and Weiner (1998) point out, GIS may be both empowering and disempowering. Marginalized groups can use GIS to stake claims to resources, advocate for changes in policies and planning, draw attention to alternative geographies and histories, and inspire more transparent and accessible decision making in government. As these technologies can be opened up to collaborative or participatory projects, GIS have the potential to be a collective force as groups organize and direct its representational prowess.

Geographic information technologies are, nonetheless, risky investments in knowledge production. As an ocular technology, GIS specifically visions from an elevated perspective. The world is displayed as seen from nowhere and everywhere. Above and disconnected, this neutralizing gaze serves to organize the world into layers of objects and actions. The risk of this disembodied visioning is the kind of distancing that it enables – subjective experiences become bounded as objects. This ocularcentrism, with the organization of space through Cartesian perspectivalism, enables an epistemology of the grid, which, as Dixon and Jones (1998: 251) write, is 'a way of knowing that imposes itself upon and eventually becomes inseparable from those processes it helps to understand'. In the context of this chapter, the use of GIS to research the city risks concretizing and elevating a specific ontology of the urban that is best analyzed by the GIS.

For your dissertation, GIS may simply be a means to an end, a method to analyze and visualize a set of data about the city. In this chapter, I have attempted to situate this technology – to show that it did not just appear out of thin air and that each stage of the research process using GIS is imbued with fundamental decisions about how to observe, measure, analyze, and represent the world. These fundamentals can be approached pragmatically – as is the goal for the use of this chapter – and such practices would take necessary steps toward an engaged and responsible use of this technology.

Frequently Asked Questions

1. I'd like to have a map of data points from my research. How do I get those points to display on the map?

Esri and many web-based mapping products allow users to add data points directly to a map. Consult the help files for the software package you are using. You should be able to add points stored as x–y data in the form of latitude–longitude. You may also have the option to add

(Continued)

(Continued)

addresses directly as points on a map using a specific tool called a geocoder.

2. What is a 'spatial reference system', and why should I care?

A spatial reference system is used as a system of measurement for a geometric object. When working with spatial data, a spatial reference system is necessary to know how to measure distances and areas. Without a properly defined spatial reference system, a researcher may not be able to overlay datasets, nor perform basic analyses.

3. I want to make my maps more interactive and on the web. Are there easy ways to do that online?

After working on your maps, you may wish to make those maps available over the Internet – on your personal website or on your blog. Beyond producing a pdf that can be downloaded, you can use websites like GeoCommons.com or ArcGIS.com to publish your data and embed interactive maps into your website.

4. I use an Apple Macintosh computer. What are my options for running GIS?

Esri's ArcGIS Desktop software runs on the Microsoft Windows operating system. As such, in order to run ArcGIS on your Macintosh, you will need to emulate Windows on your Mac using BootCamp and, perhaps, Parallels or VMware Fusion. In general, I tend to tell students that this solution can be frustrating at best, given the resource drain of the ArcGIS software. Other GIS systems like Cartographica run directly on the Mac OS. There may also be web-based GIS solutions that will suffice.

5. I tend toward more qualitative forms of engagement and inquiry. How might I use GIS?

It's entirely possible that GIS are not useful for your project. However, if geographic representations help you to explore the spatial contexts of your problem or question, or if maps are useful final products of your analysis, or if maps provide a creative tension with your interview subjects, then perhaps GIS are something to explore (see Figure 9.3).

Follow Up References

Cope, M. and Elwood, S.A. (eds) (2009) *Qualitative GIS: A Mixed Methods Approach.* London: Sage.

Qualitative GIS has become the primary text for the theory, method, and practice of alternative GIS. Operating both conceptually, to shift the imagination of GIS in society, and practically, to produce new techniques around geographic representation, this edited collection sets the stage for a renewed criticality in GIScience.

Crampton, J.W. (2010) *Mapping: A Critical Introduction to Cartography and GIS.* Malden, MA: Wiley–Blackwell.

Crampton's *Mapping* marks a coming-of-age of the critical cartography and critical GIS subfields. This text, targeted at students and faculty new to these ideas, presents the foundational concepts and origin stories for the practice of critical mapping scholarship. Here, Crampton brings the critical concepts of the GIS & Society agenda to bear on the emergence of the geoweb.

Krygier, J. and Wood, D. (2005) *Making Maps: A Visual Guide to Map Design for GIS.* New York: Guilford Press.

New to cartographic design? Start with *Making Maps*, by John Krygier and Denis Wood. They bring levity to the design decisions of map-making, beginning with basic questions around intent and audience and ending with more complicated decisions around color, visual hierarchy, balance, and use of negative space.

Schuurman, N. (2004) *GIS: A Short Introduction* (Short Introductions to Geography). Malden, MA: Blackwell.

If you are interested in learning more about the 'GIS wars' of the 1990s, the emerging GIS & Society agenda, and the perspective of GIScientists, then look at *GIS: A Short Introduction*. Drawing forward her interventions in the field beginning in the late 1990s, Schuurman presents an overview of the key concepts and techniques of GIScience in a way that appreciates a diverse audience of human geographers and social scientists more generally.

Yau, N.C. (2011) *Visualize This: The Flowing Data Guide to Design, Visualization, and Statistics.* Indianapolis, IN: Wiley.

Nathan Yau, the author of the FlowingData.com blog, pulled together *Visualize This* for a group of visualization enthusiasts who are increasingly looking to open-source, web-based technologies to present compelling graphics with 'big data'. The text presumes a kind of hacker sensibility and offers an entire chapter on web-based mapping techniques, with example scripts to be copied and pasted for your mapping projects.

References

Bodenhamer, D.J., Corrigan, J. and Harris, T.M. (eds) (2010) *The Spatial Humanities: GIS and the Future of Humanities Scholarship.* Bloomington, IN: Indiana University Press.

Brown, M. and Knopp, K. (2008) Queering the map: the productive tensions of colliding epistemologies. *Annals of the Association of American Geographers*, 98: 1–19.

Budd, L. and Adey, P. (2009) The software-simulated airworld: anticipatory code and affective aeromobilities. *Environment and Planning A*, 41: 1366–85.

Chrisman, N.R. (2002) *Exploring Geographic Information Systems* (2nd edn). New York: Wiley.

Clark, G.L. (1992) GIS – what crisis? *Environment and Planning A*, 24: 321–2.

Cooper, D. and Gregory, I.N. (2011) Mapping the English Lake District: a literary GIS. *Transactions of the Institute of British Geographers, NS*, 36: 89–108.

Cope, M. and Elwood, S.A. (eds) (2009) *Qualitative GIS: A Mixed Methods Approach.* London: Sage.

Couclelis, H. (1992) People manipulate objects (but cultivate fields): beyond the raster–vector debate in GIS. *Lecture Notes in Computer Science*, 639: 65–77.

Craig, W.J., Harris, T.M. and Weiner, D. (eds) (2002) *Community Participation and Geographic Information Systems.* New York: Taylor & Francis.

Dixon, D.P. and Jones, J.P., III (1998) My dinner with Derrida, or spatial analysis and poststructuralism do lunch. *Environment and Planning A*, 30: 247–60.

Dobson, J.E. (1993) The geographic revolution: a retrospective on the age of automated geography. *The Professional Geographer*, 45: 431–9.

Dodge, M. and Kitchin, R. (2009) Software, objects, and home space. *Environment and Planning A*, 41: 1344–65.

Dragicevic, S. and Balram, S. (eds) (2006) *Collaborative Geographic Information Systems.* Hershey, PA: Idea Group, Inc.

Elwood, S.A. (2002) GIS use in community planning: a multidimensional analysis of empowerment. *Environment and Planning A*, 34: 905–22.

Elwood, S.A. (2006) Beyond cooptation or resistance: urban spatial politics, community organizations, and GIS-based spatial narratives. *Annals of the Association of American Geographers*, 96: 323–41.

Elwood, S.A. (2009) Integrating participatory action research and GIS education: negotiating methodologies, politics and technologies. *Journal of Geography in Higher Education*, 33: 51–65.

Harris, T.M. and Weiner, D. (1998) Empowerment, marginalization, and 'community-integrated' GIS. *Cartography and Geographic Information Systems*, 25: 67–76.

Jung, J.K. (2009) Software-level integration of CAQDAS and GIS, in M. Cope and S. Elwood (eds), *Qualitative GIS: A Mixed Methods Approach.* London: Sage, pp. 115–35.

King, G. (1996) *Mapping Reality: An Exploration of Cultural Cartographies.* New York: St Martin's Press.

Knigge, L. and Cope, M. (2006) Grounded visualization: integrating the analysis of qualitative and quantitative data through grounded theory and visualization. *Environment and Planning A*, 38: 2021–37.

Kwan, M.P. (2007) Affecting geospatial technologies: toward a feminist politics of emotion. *The Professional Geographer*, 59: 27–34.

Kwan, M.P. (2008) From oral histories to visual narratives: re-presenting the post-September 11 experiences of the Muslim women in the USA. *Social and Cultural Geography*, 9: 653–69.

Lake, R.W. (1993) Planning and applied geography: positivism, ethics, and geographic information systems. *Progress in Human Geography*, 17: 404–13.

Lawson, V. (1995) The politics of difference: examining the quantitative/qualitative dualism in post–structuralist feminist research. *The Professional Geographer*, 47: 449–57.

Longley, P. (2005) Geographical Information Systems: a renaissance of geodemographics for public service delivery. *Progress in Human Geography*, 29: 57–63.

Macgill, S.M. (1990) Commentary: GIS in the 1990s? *Environment and Planning A*, 22: 1559–1560.

Nyerges, T.L. and Aguirre, R.W. (2011) Public participation in analytic-deliberative decision making: evaluating a large-group online field experiment. *Annals of the Association of American Geographers*, 103: 561–86.

Openshaw, S. (1991) A view on the GIS crisis in geography, or, using GIS to put Humpty-Dumpty back together again. *Environment and Planning A*, 23: 621–8.

Openshaw, S. (1992) Further thoughts on geography and GIS: a reply. *Environment and Planning A*, 24: 463–6.

Pavlovskaya, M. (2004) Other transitions: multiple economies of Moscow households in the 1990s. *Annals of the Association of American Geographers*, 94: 329–51.

Pavlovskaya, M. (2009) Non-quantitative GIS, in M. Cope and S. Elwood (eds), *Qualitative GIS: A Mixed Methods Approach*. London: Sage, pp. 13–37.

Pickles, J. (1993) Discourse on method and the history of discipline: reflections on Dobson's 1983 Automated Geography. *The Professional Geographer*, 45: 451–5.

Pickles, J. (ed.) (1995) *Ground Truth: The Social Implications of Geographic Information Systems*. New York: Guilford.

Pickles, J. (2006) Ground truth, 1995–2005. *Transactions in GIS*, 10: 763–72.

Schuurman, N. (2000) Trouble in the heartland: GIS and its critics in the 1990s. *Progress in Human Geography*, 24: 569–90.

Schuurman, N. (2006) Formalization matters: critical GIS and ontology research. *Annals of the Association of American Geographers*, 96: 726–39.

Sheppard, E. (1995) GIS and society: towards a research agenda. *Cartography and Geographic Information Systems*, 22: 5–16.

Sheppard, E. (2005) Knowledge production through critical GIS: genealogy and prospects. *Cartographica*, 40: 5–21.

Smith, N. (1992) History and philosophy of geography: real wars, theory wars. *Progress in Human Geography*, 16: 257–71.

Stanford University Libraries (2006) *Guidelines for Finding GIS Data*. Stanford University, 16 March. Available from www-sul.stanford.edu/depts/gis/FindData.html (accessed August 2011).

Talen, E. (2000) Bottom-up GIS: a new tool for individual and group expression in participatory planning. *Journal of the American Planning Association*, 66: 279–94.

Taylor, P.J. (1990) GKS. *Political Geography Quarterly*, 9: 211–12.

Taylor, P.J. and Overton, M. (1991) Further thoughts on geography and GIS. *Environment and Planning A*, 23: 1087–90.

Thrift, N. (2004) Remembering the technological unconscious by foregrounding knowledges of position. *Environment and Planning D: Society and Space*, 22: 175–90.

Wilson, M.W. (2009) Towards a genealogy of qualitative GIS, in M. Cole and S. Elwood (eds), *Qualitative GIS: A Mixed Methods Approach*. London: Sage, pp. 156–70.

Wilson, M.W. (2011a) 'Training the eye': formation of the geocoding subject. *Social and Cultural Geography*, 12: 357–76.

Wilson, M.W. (2011b) Data matter(s): legitimacy, coding, and qualifications-of-life. *Environment and Planning D: Society and Space*, 29: 857–72.

Wood, D. (1992) *The Power of Maps*. New York: Guilford Press.

Yau, N.C. (2011) *Visualize This: The Flowing Data Guide to Design, Visualization, and Statistics*. Indianapolis, IN: Wiley.

Yuan, M. (2010) Mapping text, in J. Bodenhamer, T.M. Corrigan and M. Harris (eds), *The Spatial Humanities: GIS and the Future of Humanities Scholarship*. Bloomington, IN: Indiana University Press, pp. 109–23.

Zook, M.A. and Graham, M. (2007) The creative reconstruction of the Internet: Google and the privatization of cyberspace and DigiPlace. *Geoforum*, 38: 1322–43.

Zook, M.A., Graham, M., Shelton, T. and Gorman, S. (2010) Volunteered geographic information and crowdsourcing disaster relief: a case study of the Haitian earthquake. *World Medical & Health Policy*, 2: 7–33.

10
WORLDS THROUGH GLASS: PHOTOGRAPHY AND VIDEO AS GEOGRAPHIC METHOD

Bradley L. Garrett

Introduction to glass geographies

Photography and video are two methods often paired under a banner of 'visual methodologies' within geography (Rose 2001). While both methods share the ability to capture and relay images, and making still and moving images often can now be accomplished with a single piece of equipment, the process of preparation, utilization, processing and dissemination are, in fact, quite different, given that video captures motion and sound as well as images. In this chapter I will discuss using both photography and video, identifying points of crossover where possible, to unpack the merits and pitfalls of each through my ethnographic work with urban explorers, where I have used media methods extensively.

It must be said, as a starting point, that much of the engagement geography has had with photography and video has been in the context of studying images produced by others, be it in an archive (Brickell and Garrett 2013; Rose 2000) or in more popular contexts (Aitken and Zonn 1994; Cresswell and Dixon 2002; Curti 2008). While those studies are interesting and useful, this chapter, in terms of method, is focused purely on media *production* rather than *analysis* (Bauch 2010; Sidaway 2002), with the researcher, often alongside project participants, taking on the role of media maker. I am interested in photography and video work as *being* and *doing*, a process of engagement and interaction with the world around us in ways that meld and blur representations and practice. Therefore, I suggest, the process of making photos and videos is just as important as what we do with them. For those of you reading this chapter as a guide to using 'visual' methods in the process of, for instance, putting together your dissertation, I hope you will find it a useful starting point to using those methods effectively and critically.

The title of this chapter implies that mediation takes place when we see worlds *through* glass, that the world is filtered through the lens. While that is true, we also now live our lives through glass, on screen, through other people, through emotional filters, social and cultural sieves – in other words, life is a morphing, complicated meld of human and machine, culture and biology, analogue and digital – it is all at once hybrid (Haraway 1991; Whatmore 2002). Technological devices like cameras, and what we choose do with them, are a part of our daily existence, wrapped up in the choices we make and desires we harbour in every moment of every day, especially now that those machines are almost always on our bodies (and likely soon in them). Photographs and videos 'are not something that appear over and against reality, but parts of practices through which people work to establish realities' (Crang 1997: 362). Those realities are part of who we are as people, part of our sociality, part of our culture, and as researchers it is our role to engage with them critically. While photography and video now are part of our daily lives, the way we use them as research tools should be quite different to the way we use them at home, in setting up, recording and dissemination of those media. Think about the ways in which photography and video might be used in your work. Consider the ranges of scale, differing contexts and innovative ways you might apply these methods.

In this chapter, I will make three important points in the context of audio/visual research. The first is that video and photography are utilized and conceptualized in quite different ways as research tools, even as they both become more common, accepted and appreciated. I will try to bridge the practices where I can, given that many students may want to try using both on research projects. Second, I will suggest that video and photos, now more than ever, are part of a process of creating worlds, not simple representations of them. Researchers should and do play an active role in the production and reproduction of those media cultures even as they interrogate them. Finally, I will make it clear that now is the perfect time for geographers to confront long-held concerns around the 'occularcentrism' (Jay 1993), 'masculine gazes' (Rose 2001) or 'touristic gazes' (Urry 1990) of visual methods by directly confronting the ways in which we wield these methods (Driver 2003). As undergraduate or graduate researchers, you perhaps have more facility with these methods than many established geography researchers. This puts you in a strong position to lead the way in their use.

As Bauch has written, visual media, especially video, are 'socially ubiquitous yet almost awkwardly absent' from geography (Bauch 2010: 475). What will become clear by the end of the chapter, however, is that this is changing quickly: visual methods are being rapidly deployed across the social sciences (Garrett 2010b; Jewitt 2011) and will inevitably become a vital part of what geographers do; it is up to new generations of researchers – such as you – to define the terms of engagement. There are also dangers here that need be addressed – the potential pitfalls of working with these methods. Using them uncritically gets us into ethical, legal and logistical deep water very quickly. Some of these issues, which we will explore here, have been negotiated by other social sciences (Erickson 2011). Other problems are, perhaps, unique to geography. The final take-away point is that photography and video are not 'shortcut' methods; they are sensitive, difficult work.

Initiating a process of doing research using video and/or photography is not ever as simple as just 'packing a camera' and heading out. The process of making image and sound recordings of people is a highly sensitive and politically charged issue. It is therefore very important that, as a potential media researcher, you put a great deal of thought behind what it is you intend to do with those devices, making objectives clear to the people you are working with.

Kitting up – preparing for research

As part of my PhD research I produced more than 12,000 still images and recorded more than 60 hours of video footage. I published this material on my blog, on Flickr, Vimeo, Facebook and YouTube, and used those recordings for presentations and publications in many different contexts. In the process of my work I undertook a wide 'visual ethnography', using four still cameras, four video cameras and various types of note taking, creating a multimodal, multisensual, multimedia ethnography intended to integrate more of the embodied experience of the research process into the final product (Herbert, 2000). This process, while deeply rewarding, was long, arduous, even tedious at times, and is not readily reflected in the polished final products available online. In this first section of preparing for research, I would like to unravel a bit of what goes on outside the frame when setting up a research project of this sort. Set-up and learning curve are two things you need to consider carefully – particularly as I had three years to do my PhD while you may have only a matter of months to do your dissertation!

As a self-confessed technophile, I would love to suggest that preparing to do glass geographies begins with choosing the right equipment. It doesn't: it begins with intention. Before embarking on any research project, you must first confront the fundamental question of whether media methods are appropriate for what you intend to do (see Chapter 2, this volume). In many instances creating recordings of people, places and events can be seen as threatening or exploitative and the last thing you want to do, as a researcher, is close doors before you even begin because you chose a method based on your preference or desire rather than for the appropriateness to the situation. For my colleague Erika Sigvardsdotter, who works with undocumented persons in Sweden, taking images of her project participants could actually endanger their lives or livelihoods, should they be published or shared inappropriately (Sigvardsdotter 2012). This may seem counterintuitive to those of us used to being photographed and filmed almost constantly, and indeed many of her project participants enjoyed being photographed, but the social, cultural and political implications of making media records is a necessary point of interrogation. That said, photography and video can, equally, be empowering and open doors for a researcher. Hester Parr, who has done extensive work with the homeless and mentally ill, follows Sara Kindon (2003) when she writes that 'video work can reduce the "distance" between researcher and researched and destabilize power relations in this relationship in ways that facilitate research that "makes a difference"' (Parr 2007: 115). Both Kindon and Parr have undertaken research from a participatory angle, bringing the 'researched' into the production process. In this context, as Mike Crang argues, video, as well as photography, is 'a research tool that is socially embedded and closes the gap of representation and practice' (Crang 1997: 365).

Turning back to my own experience, I conducted an audio/visual ethnography with urban explorers in London over the course of three years (Garrett 2010a; Garrett 2011; Garrett 2013). Urban explorers recreationally trespass into derelict, obsolete, temporary and infrastructural places in cities. Many urban explorers are exceptional photographers, producing stunning low-light, long-exposure photographs that they have become widely known for (see Figure 10.1), and they are used to having cameras around them, if not necessarily trained on them.

However, the implications of photographing and video recording us undertaking unauthorised activity together was quite serious. When I initially approached the community, I offered to produce a documentary film about the practice, thinking it

Figure 10.1 Brad and Marc Explo at Unibrow

would be seen as a valuable addition to the photography work already thriving within it. However, when many participants made it clear they were not comfortable being filmed (especially with me filming access details to places we explored), I decided to purchase a still camera so that I could better blend with the photography culture I was studying and, at the least, get some photos for my thesis. Little did I know that I would end up learning far more about photography than I ever expected; and many of my project participants, after seeing my enthusiasm for video as well as photography (I eventually carried both cameras everywhere), not only got excited about my video productions, they also used my equipment (and their own) to take over the production! In the end, the research process took off in all sorts of unexpected directions. The important point here is that when I realized my methods were slightly inappropriate, I changed them. On your dissertation you may have much less time than I did and quite possibly will not be able to change tack. Again, careful consideration of which techniques are going to work best before beginning your fieldwork are vital. Know who you are working with and what might make them uncomfortable. Know what you intend to do with the resulting images after fieldwork is 'done' and talk to your project participants about it. Most universities will have ethics and risk assessment guidelines that you should read and adhere to whilst doing your dissertations, and these are helpful templates. That is not to say you shouldn't push those boundaries: sometimes you have to and should, but be clear about what you are doing and why. Sketch out a rough plan for your project from beginning to end, paying close attention to those ethical sticking points (Chapter 2, this volume).

Let us now consider what you might do with your cameras, and what tools will be best for the job. Often, you will use more than one camera. Sarah Pink argues convincingly that there is some case to be made for obtaining as many forms of records as possible, as she did on a walking tour of a Cittàslow town, collecting 'multi-sensorial and multi-modal experience ... represented with different intensity in different media' (Pink 2008: 190). Spinney (2009) and Brown et al. (2008) have done interesting work using head-mounted video cameras, which can be used in conjunction with other media, to capture first-person perspectives of events. I used a similar technique for parts of a 2010 film called *London's Olympic Waterscape* where we took the viewer on a recorded 'triathlon' around the under-construction 2012 Olympic stadium (Anton et al. 2012). In other cases, such as in Laurier and Philo's work in an Edinburgh café (Laurier and Philo 2006a) and Paul Simpson's work as a busker in Bath (Simpson 2011), a static shot from a fixed video camera can capture moments that the researcher may have missed or wished not to be present for. Your choice of lens (thinking about the width of the frame and zoom capabilities) may also greatly affect how much of the scene is captured and there are important implications to framing a shot to be considered – what and who is going to be in and out of frame and why? What will you choose to be in focus? Each of these decisions have important implications. Finally, whatever you choose, make sure you leave yourself enough time to get comfortable with your equipment before you go into the field.

Video footage can, in some instances, replace written records where the primary goal is to record non-verbal communication such as subtle eye movements and body language (Laurier and Philo 2006b). Alasuutari (1995: 43) writes that 'to record non-verbal communication one needs a movie or video camera, and in a group discussion situation there should probably be several of them'. The multiple gazes of multiple cameras, as well as strategically placed microphones, might capture what your eyes did not, especially if you were staring at a notebook. In a participatory video environment, a digital camera where you can show people images you have taken in the field may be crucial. In my work with urban explorers, learning to take decent digital photographs quickly and being able to review and discuss them after an exploration was vital to be able to participate in the culture.

It is important to keep in mind that video, unlike photography, also records sound. This can be very useful in, for instance, getting people to speak candidly while recording with the lens cap on (collecting no visuals) and in thinking about how audio recording can be used separately and in conjunction with images. On a project I undertook with Brian Rosa and Jonathan Prior in Dundee, Scotland, we decided to make a film that foregrounded audio rather than visuals. Jonathan, who worked with audio recording as part of his research method, collected sound on a professional recorder using various microphones while Brian and I shot video, often without sound. The result, *Jute*, is a film as much about what you hear as what you see (Garrett et al. 2011) and challenges the implied 'visuality' of video (Crang 2003).

On long road trips during my urban exploration project, I took inexpensive disposable still cameras that I put in multiple pockets so I always had one within reach at a moment's notice. I also gave them to my project participants and asked them to

Figure 10.2 The crew heading underground in Paris

photograph whatever they wanted. Often they photographed me. We threw those cameras around, took technically horrible pictures of each other and broke or lost a few of them. Seemingly half of the pictures didn't turn out. However, those photos and memories, looking back on them now, are more important to me than I ever could have imagined. Viewing them triggers the feelings, flashes and fleeting associations that made up my time in the field (see Figure 10.2) and are far more important, in many ways, than the beautiful 'formal' images I took with my more expensive digital cameras.

In other instances, my large shoulder-mounted, broadcast-quality video camera could get me into places or get me an interview I would not have otherwise been able to land, since I looked 'professional' – the role of 'cameraperson' here playing out a 'double game which consists [of] acting in conformity with one's interests while giving the appearance of playing by the rules' (Bourdieu and Lamaison 1986: 113). Crang and Cook (2007: 43) point out:

> Some researchers have found that activities such as photography … can provide a readily understood reason and purpose for their presence in certain places at certain times. At tourist sites, weddings or historical reenactments, for example, someone hanging around taking photographs will not stand out in a crowd.

So, in choosing equipment, consider what *roles* you want to play as well as what technical abilities you require.

Before leaving for fieldwork, I spent a great deal of time practising filming and photographing in low light conditions, learning to identify buttons on my cameras by touch alone (sometimes gluing grains of rice on buttons or wrapping tape around one

Figure 10.3 Two-week field kit

zoom ring to help with tactile identification), packing and repacking my bag to make sure I knew where everything was intuitively and checking that I had all the necessary batteries, cables, cleaning cloths, memory cards, lights and tripod equipment. While my gear all fits in a backpack (Figure 10.3), glass methods do require a lot of 'kit' and it is easy to forget a battery or memory card. Methodical organization really is essential because once you leave, often there is no going back and you may not be able to find a Nikon D90 battery car charger in rural Poland (don't ask).

Make it or break it! Doing research

Despite my (probably by now obvious) preference for video, I cannot over-emphasize the importance of the role photography played on my urban explorers project. As a result of my project participants teaching me photography, I was able to pull from multiple media for recall, from pictures and video for images, from audio for 'field interviews' (much of my footage in the London and Paris sewers ended up being too dark to see much), as well as from field notes where I scribbled thoughts while shooting. Although I am reluctant to call my work a 'visual ethnography' since it was so much *more* than visual, I felt very content in my creation of multimedia documents constructed from text, photos, audio and video because that is a reflection of what the project had been in the 'real world'. Again, 'the photograph always carries its referent with it' (Barthes 1982: 5). These recordings are markers to experiences and are imbued with memory, associations and emotions, a lot of which are not immediately obvious. However, any attempt at representation, including the written word, will be guilty of that; it is not a particularly 'visual' pitfall. Remind yourself that you are not there to 'collect data' or 'create representations' of things and events, that you are working with the 'media as practice rather than representation, as taking part in the world rather than reflecting it' (Crang, 1997: 360), will serve you well. If you have chosen your medium/media to suit your project, practising it should break the ice, bring you closer and bridge gaps.

If you find your tools are getting in the way of your research, get rid of them! As an example, two of my project participants and myself found ourselves at 3 am perched over a ventilation shaft with a 30 metre drop in Belgium, securing ropes to abseil into the never-completed Antwerp metro system with a thunderstorm rolling in. I was photographing the rope setup for my thesis as a sort of 'photography of action', creating 2- to 3- second shots of Winch and 'Gary' tying the ropes and dropping in (Figures 10.4 and 10.5).

Winch, as he was threading loops and clipping carabineers, looked straight at me and said 'Will you put down that camera and help us with these ropes, mate?' Never had my outsider status been so evident while acting as an ethnographic photographer. I put the camera away and helped, and then harnessed up and dropped in the shaft, camera safely tucked away.

Figure 10.4 'Gary' and Winch tying off ropes to abseil into the Antwerp Premetro

Figure 10.5 'Gary' abseils into the Antwerp Premetro

My project participants also often commented on the fact that I was not photographing the same things as them. LutEx, another explorer, noted that I was 'always taking pictures of people taking pictures'. Silent Motion once said to me,

PHOTOGRAPHY AND VIDEO AS GEOGRAPHIC METHOD

'I like how your pictures look like they're in motion, they are of us actually *doing* exploration'. As anthropologist Sol Worth writes, 'film (and photography) is not so much about what is "out there" as what is "in here"' (Worth 1981, cited in Crang and Cook 2007: 112), and my photographs revealed active processes of being and doing as much as it created the staged experiential representations urban explorers are known for.

While some have argued that photography is 'an act of non-intervention' (Sontag 1977: 11), I found that it became very much a part of me and brought me closer to the action. The best advice I ever received in terms of shooting video, and this easily applies to shooting photography, is to follow Rouch and Feld (2003) in conceiving of the camera as an appendage to the body. Capturing images, after making those initial rational decisions about what to use, when, where and why, is far more felt than thought. An ethnographic film instructor I took a class with called Mike Yorke told me that in India, where he shot a film about holy men and women in 2008, the Sadhus said he did 'camera yoga', impossibly bending around obstacles, walking backward, controlling his breathing and holding a heavy camera for hours on end. Filming and photographing project participants becomes a dance, where you run and scramble to get shots and they work to screw them up, act up for them or ignore you. After a time 'camera intimidation', which may keep them from acting 'normally', dissipates if you have chosen your method wisely and wield it with grace and confidence. On my project, after I started shooting video a few people asked not to be filmed (even when they were happy to be photographed), so I simply cut them out of frame or edited them out in postproduction (more on this in the following section) where necessary. It wasn't a big issue here, though that is not to say on another project it might not be more of a sticking point or even totally inappropriate. Again, consult your university guidelines and speak with your instructor about what might and might not be suitable.

Before we move on to the next section I want to emphasize that in your methodological framework the intentionality that you are carrying from beginning to end should be serving you in the field. It is best not to haphazardly record everything that is happening, though if you are working on a very limited time frame (a weekend perhaps where you are recording an event), it may make more sense to do so. Keep in mind that everything you collect will have to be transferred, organized, edited, stored and shared (Snell 2011). As a general rule, one day of photography will require one day to process, and one day of videography will require three days to process. I collected 60 hours of video footage during my PhD work and spent over 180 hours going through it and compiling rough edits. In total, I spent more than 3,000 hours collecting, sorting, editing and organizing almost four terabytes of recordings and it was, as much as I loved my research topic, quite painful. Although it is unlikely you will make the same mistake on a more short-term project, do keep these thoughts in mind every time you hit the shutter/record button.

Honing media – what to do with all this stuff

Now that you have collected a bunch of recordings, you will need to sort through and organize them. Do so carefully and then back up everything twice. Put a second backup drive with everything on it in a different location or in a data cloud (not a physical location). This is not paranoia; it is the reality of working with digital media. In the event you have your bag stolen with your laptop (first copy) and hard drive (backup) inside, you will have just lost all of your work. I have three copies of every-thing that automatically back up hourly and it has saved me a number of times. Do keep in mind that universities do not grant extensions for 'lost' work and you are not going to receive preferential treatment for choosing to use a method more complicated to capture and organize.

Editing photos is relatively straightforward unless you want to start doing more creative work like layering, prints and montage. Adobe Lightroom, for instance, is a great tool for organizing and adjusting exposure, colour saturation, cropping, rotat-ing and the like. For video editing, simple programs may do, but it is also well worth obtaining something more versatile like Final Cut Pro (Mac), Avid (PC) or Adobe Premiere (Mac and PC). Once you have laid out your timeline and begun dropping in video, audio and still photos, the possibilities are innumerable. Nicholas Bauch, when writing about the production of his geography film *Across Space: Finding the Farm in the City*, writes that 'it was a constant maneuvering, shifting, manipulating, and changing of voice, audio, and visual clips to make what I thought would relay the academic aims of the project' (Bauch 2010: 479). It is easy to lose yourself in editing, just like writing. Be sure you have in mind what it is you want to relay, even as you let the intuition guide you through the creative process.

Keep in mind that the images you produce will not be passively consumed; you must remain critically aware of the decisions you are making. Good instructors will question you on why you framed an image a particular way, why you hit the record button when you did, why you edited film in a certain sequence. Keep in mind there is a critical geography behind every decision, both in the field and in the lab – expect those issues to be teased out in the analysis of your work. Your project par-ticipants, should you have any, are also likely to have concerns about how they are represented. You could use some of your time in the field to negotiate and discuss these issues with them, looking for gaps, triggering new ideas, provoking unexpected memories, and layering up your research. This type of engagement with photos is often referred to as photo elicitation – using photos to trigger discussion (Harper, 2002). Video can also be used in this way by filming yourself reviewing footage with project participants (should you have time for a return visit).

As should now be clear, taking on a project such as this will be challenging. How-ever, your role as an emerging visual researcher is a vital one. You should feel con-fident that the use of photography and video will become increasingly ubiquitous and encouraged over time; it is simply of a matter of students and instructors broaching the topic and getting out there to do the work. It is important that we now make the production of video, audio and photography just as valid a form of scholarly output as text in academia. There are new potentials to produce entire video and audio articles, photo-essays and even as-yet unimagined creative forms that critically interrogate the world around us in new and exciting ways. But these steps require us to continue pushing the envelope of utilization and critical examination of these methods and you have a key role in that.

As Mike Crang writes in *Cultural Geographies*, 'literature is ... just one creative "media" [*sic*] through which cultural ideas are produced and reproduced' (Crang, 1998: 81), and new forms of, and growing interest in, scholarship discussing the importance of video and photography should reinforce our desire to use, experiment with and disseminate those media where possible. As an academic community, we depend on each generation to push those boundaries further and it should be clear from this chapter that there is no better time than now to do so. The best way to learn about the merits and pitfalls of these methods, as with any, is through firsthand experience.

The golden age of digital media geography

Photography and video are ubiquitous tools and practices with which people define themselves and their worlds. As a result, while images proliferate and we become increasingly enraptured by them, we are also becoming more suspicious of them. As scholars and students, it is our role to interrogate the modes of conceptualizing, producing and utilizing media, new and old. Putting ourselves in that productive role places us in a much stronger position to then see the strengths and weaknesses more clearly. As should be clear now, there is no right or wrong way to do glass geographies, but there are more or less engaged and informed ways of practising them and there are methods that can quickly overproduce material. Use them critically and carefully.

Although I used both photography and video on my own research project and understand others will do the same, it is difficult to write about them as conjoined methods. They are as related, perhaps, as film and text, meaning they share characteristics (like narrative, structure and editing process) but the goals, practice and dissemination of each can be quite different. This is, of course, rapidly changing with technological shifts and media convergences (Jenkins 2006). Where once posting video online was expensive and cumbersome, it is now largely free and simple. Equipment is becoming less expensive and increasingly easy to manage. During my explorations I regularly carried two or more cameras and switched between them, often while sneaking through windows and running from security guards. It was not easy. If I had to do it all again, I would have sold all my cameras to purchase a digital single-lens reflex (DSLR) camera that also shot high definition (HD) video, investing everything in one piece of equipment with a lot of extra memory cards and batteries. Whatever you choose to use to undertake your visual geography, just make sure you know it well and enjoy using it. And of course, be prepared to lose and break it!

The most important thing to keep in mind here is that a piece of technology will not solve your problems or do your fieldwork for you. Some of the best photo work I have seen from projects comes from people's mobile phones – because they were in the right place at the right time. What matters most is that the researcher saw the opportunity and took it. Be brave with your glass geographies; ask people if you can record them, work with them to create something they appreciate and enjoy, and spend the time to work with instructors and other students to carefully unpack what you did and why you did it. New advances in digital technologies are changing the nature of geography every day and increasingly video and photography are being seen as exciting ways to get involved with the world around us. All that is left now is for you to take the lead on what future worlds through glass will look like!

Frequently Asked Questions

1. What are the benefits of photography and video?

First, photography and video can give viewers an excellent sense of space and place. It is much easier to show a clip of your research than to describe it. Using still and moving images and/or audio also allows you to work more creatively, trying out new ways of recording and presenting information. Photography and video can also empower the people you work with, allowing them to speak for themselves or take over the production, rather than having you (as an 'expert') speak for them. These methods are also very useful for sharing your research online. Finally, they are fun!

2. Should I use photography or video on my project?

Your choice of method is very important and you want to first consider whether either is appropriate. If you will be working in strenuous field conditions where a camera will be a hindrance or in a situation where people may be uncomfortable with it, consider another method. However, if you are deciding between photography and video, remember that photographs take less hard drive space

(Continued)

(Continued)

and are easier to store, manipulate and edit but video will give you motion and sound in addition to images.

3. When are these methods inappropriate?

Generally I would say that if your method, whatever it happens to be, makes your project participants uncomfortable, you should think carefully about using it. Even if you do not have any human participants, in other cases, such as on private property, you may also run into issues about photographing what some people will see as 'off-limits' or 'sensitive'. Think about this before you go out to do your research and consult with your instructor and university guidelines for media practice.

4. What kind of camera should I buy/use?

Here you need to balance the technical requirement you need (do you need it to shoot photos in low light? Do you want your video to be broadcast quality? Do you need to hook up an external microphone for better sound?) with the application of the technology. In some instances, a smaller camera will do the job and is easier to travel with and less troubling if broken or lost. In other cases, a larger, more professional camera may lend you some appearance of legitimacy that opens doors. Also think about how you will store and work with these images. Do you have access to enough space and a powerful enough computer to edit high definition video for instance? Be sure you weigh all these options – don't just run out and buy the newest technology.

5. Where can I get more information on using photography and video?

I would suggest Sarah Pink's book *Doing Visual Ethnography: Images, Media and Representation in Research* as a good starting point. For a more geographic perspective, Gillian Rose's book *Visual Methodologies: An Introduction to the Interpretation of Visual Material* is also very good. Finally, I have written an article in the journal *Progress in Human Geography* entitled 'Videographic geographies: using digital video for geographic research' which covers the different types of video work and their applications. Details of all three are in the follow up references below.

Follow Up References

Bauch, N. (2010) The academic geography video genre: a methodological examination. *Geography Compass,* 4/5: 475–84.

This article complements the video 'Across space: finding the farm in the city'. It first outlines key methodological considerations in the production of a video in the academic geography video genre, including technology, scripting, editing and the implications of authorship related to each of these. Then it discusses the intellectual aims of the video, which are to (i) show where the farm is represented in the city, (ii) show that by using the categories of urban and rural it allows us to attach values to places of a certain character, sometimes unjustifiably so, and (iii) demonstrate the transformative properties of space, that is, how the meanings of artefacts change when they are used in different spatial contexts. The article concludes with methodological suggestions for other videographers wishing to produce motion pictures that relate themes frequently undertaken in academic geography.

Downing, M.J. and Tenney, L.J. (2008) *Video Vision: Changing the Culture of Social Science Research.* Newcastle upon Tyne: Cambridge Scholars Publishing.

In this volume Downing and Tenney zoom in on ethics, methodology and analysis, while also zooming out on a wider praxis. They argue that the time is here to collectively identify our experiences, methods and knowledge of video as a research methodology. This compilation of work unpacks the use of video as a research tool. Often through the interdisciplinary lens of environmental psychology as well as anthropology, sociology and the broader field of psychology, fascinating angles of the use of participant and naturalistic observations are captured along with that of participatory action research. Strategies such as recording video messages, the creation of student-informed videos and facilitating videos taken by or edited by research participants are coupled with methods for obtaining institutional review board approvals, analysis, development of theory or action and presentation. This volume presents thought-provoking, cutting-edge research that is both accessible to students and useful for social scientists who are yearning for a more accurate way to collect, analyse, and present data in our hyper-technical, visual and competitive world.

Garrett, B.L. (2010) Videographic geographies: using digital video for geographic research. *Progress in Human Geography,* 35: 521–41.

This article is a review of the ways in which human geography has engaged with film and video. Beginning with a look at the history of cinematic analysis within the discipline, the paper outlines different possible uses for digital video, focusing on its merits as a multisensory ethnographic method. The article encourages geographers to make the move from analysis to production, citing examples from successful recent projects that have done so, endorsing further integration of video

PHOTOGRAPHY AND VIDEO AS GEOGRAPHIC METHOD

into fieldwork and an increase in digital publication to create what we might call videographic geographies.

Garrett, B.L. (2010) Urban explorers: quests for myth, mystery and meaning. *Geography Compass*, 4/5: 1448–61.

This article is the practical extension of this chapter. It is about urban exploration, a cultural practice of exploring derelict, closed and normally inaccessible built environments. The article is, in a sense, an experiment in research, learning and representation and is as much about the way the information is presented as it is about the topic itself. It consists of two parts. The first component is a video article that can be viewed online at http://vimeo.com/5366045. The second is this document, an annotated script and short article meant to support the videographic document. The piece, as a whole, is a review of the work of five scholars (Alastair Bonnett, Tim Edensor, Caitlin DeSilvey, Hayden Lorimer and David Pinder) who have studied the theories and practices behind contemporary urban exploration from a number of different perspectives. I include video footage of my own ethnographic research on the topic, though I allow discussion of previous work to contextualize those images to establish what might be considered a videographic literature review.

Rose, G. (2001) *Visual Methodologies: An Introduction to the Interpretation of Visual Materials.* Thousand Oaks, CA: Sage.

This book is an introduction to reading visual culture. It explains which methods are available to the undergraduate student and shows exactly how to use them. The book begins with a discussion of general themes and recent debates on the meaning of culture and the function of the visual that offers a critical inquiry into the relation of visual images to social identities and social relations. Rose then goes on to investigate in detail the different methods for interpreting visual images. The strengths and weaknesses of each method are discussed in relation to a detailed case study, as well as to the more general issues outlined in the introduction.

Pink, S. (2007) *Doing Visual Ethnography: Images, Media and Representation in Research.* Manchester: Manchester University Press in association with the Granada Centre for Visual Anthropology.

This book explores the use and potential of photography, video and hypermedia in ethnographic and social research. It offers a reflexive approach to theoretical, methodological, practical and ethical issues of using these media now that they are increasingly being incorporated into field research. Pink adopts the viewpoint that visual research methods should be rooted in a critical understanding of local and academic visual cultures, the visual media, and technologies being used, and the ethical issues they raise.

References

Aitken, S.C. and Zonn, L. (1994) *Place, Power, Situation, and Spectacle: A Geography of Film.* Lanham, MD: Rowman & Littlefield.

Alasuutari, P. (1995) *Researching Culture: Qualitative Method and Cultural Studies.* Thousand Oaks, CA: Sage.

Anton, M., Garrett, B.L., Hess, A., Miles, E. and Moreau, T. (2012) London's Olympic waterscape: capturing transition. *International Journal of Heritage Studies,* 19 (2): 125–38.

Barthes, R. (1982) *Camera Lucida.* New York: Hill and Wang.

Bauch, N. (2010) The academic geography video genre: a methodological examination. *Geography Compass,* May: 475–84.

Bourdieu, P. and Lamaison, P. (1986) From rules to strategies: an interview with Pierre Bourdieu. *Cultural Anthropology,* 1: 110–20.

Brickell, K. and Garrett, B.L. (2013) Geography, film and exploration: women and amateur filmmaking in the Himalayas. *Transactions of the Institute of British Geographers,* 38: 7–11.

Brown, K.M., Dilley, R. and Marshall, K. (2008) Using a head-mounted video camera to understand social worlds and experiences. *Sociological Research Online,* 13: 1.

Crang, M. (1997) Picturing practices: research through the tourist gaze. *Progress in Human Geography,* 21: 359–73.

Crang, M. (1998) *Cultural Geography.* New York: Routledge.

Crang, M. (2003) The hair in the gate: visuality and geographical knowledge. *Antipode,* 35: 238–43.

Crang, M. and Cook, I. (2007) *Doing Ethnographies.* London: Sage.

Cresswell, T. and Dixon, D. (2002) *Engaging Film: Geographies of Mobility and Identity.* Lanham, MD: Rowman & Littlefield.

Curti, G.H. (2008) The ghost in the city and a landscape of life: a reading of difference in Shirow and Oshii's Ghost in the Shell. *Environment and Planning D: Society and Space,* 26: 87–106.

Driver, F. (2003) On geography as a visual discipline. *Antipode,* 35: 227–31.

Erickson, F. (2011) Uses of video in social research: a brief history. *International Journal of Social Research Methodology,* 14: 179–89.

Garrett, B.L. (2010a) Urban explorers: quests for myth, mystery and meaning. *Geography Compass,* 4: 1448–61.

Garrett, B.L. (2010b) Videographic geographies: using digital video for geographic research. *Progress in Human Geography,* 35: 521–41.

Garrett, B.L. (2011) Assaying history: creating temporal junctions through urban exploration. *Environment and Planning D: Society and Space,* 29: 1048–67.

Garrett, B.L. (2013) Undertaking recreational trespass: an ethnography of urban exploration. *Transactions of the Institute of British Geographers,* Doi: 10.111/tran./2001.

Garrett, B.L., Rosa, B. and Prior, J. (2011) Jute: excavating material and symbolic surfaces. *Liminalities: A Journal of Performance Studies,* 7: 1–4.

Haraway, D.J. (1991) *Simians, Cyborgs and Women: The Reinvention of Nature.* London: Routledge.

Harper, D. (2002) Talking about pictures: a case for photo elicitation. *Visual Studies*, 17: 13–27.

Herbert, S. (2000) For ethnography. *Progress in Human Geography*, 24: 550–68.

Jay, M. (1993) Ideology and ocularcentrism: is there anything behind the mirror's tain?, in M. Jay (ed.), *Force Fields: Between Intellectual History and Cultural Critique*. London: Routledge, pp. 134–46.

Jenkins, H. (2006) *Convergence Culture: Where Old and New Media Collide*. New York: New York University Press.

Jewitt, C. (2011) Editorial. *International Journal of Social Research Methodology*, 14: 171–8.

Kindon, S. (2003) Participatory video in geographic research: a feminist practice of looking? *Area*, 35: 142–53.

Laurier, E. and Philo, C. (2006a) Possible geographies: a passing encounter in a café. *Area*, 38: 353–63.

Laurier, E. and Philo, C. (2006b) Cold shoulders and napkins handed: gestures of responsibility. *Transactions of the Institute of British Geographers*, 31 (2): 193–207.

Parr, H. (2007) Collaborative film-making as process, method and text in mental health research. *Cultural Geographies*, 14: 114–38.

Pink, S. (2008) An urban tour: the sensory sociality of ethnographic place-making. *Ethnography*, 9: 175–96.

Rose, G. (2000) Practising photography: an archive, a study, some photographs and a researcher. *Journal of Historical Geography*, 26: 555–71.

Rose, G. (2001) *Visual Methodologies: An Introduction to the Interpretation of Visual Materials*. Thousand Oaks, CA: Sage.

Rouch, J. and Feld, S. (2003) *Cine-Ethnography (Visible Evidence)*. Minneapolis, MN: University of Minnesota Press.

Sidaway, J. (2002) Photography as geographical fieldwork. *Journal of Geography in Higher Education*, 26: 95–103.

Sigvardsdotter, E. (2012) *Presenting the Absent: An Account of Undocumentedness in Sweden*. Uppsala: Uppsala University Department of Social and Economic Geography.

Simpson, P. (2011) 'So, as you can see ...': some reflections on the utility of video methodologies in the study of embodied practices. *Area*, 43: 343–52.

Snell, J. (2011) Interrogating video data: systematic quantitative analysis versus micro-ethnographic analysis. *International Journal of Social Research Methodology*, 14: 253–58.

Sontag, S. (1977) *On Photography*. New York: Picador.

Spinney, J. (2009) Cycling the city: movement, meaning and method. *Geography Compass*, 3: 817–35.

Urry, J. (1990) *The Tourist Gaze: Leisure and Travel in Contemporary Societies*. London: Sage.

Whatmore, S. (2002) *Hybrid Geographies: Natures, Cultures, Spaces*. Thousand Oaks, CA: Sage.

Worth, S. (1981) *Studying Visual Communication: Selected Writings*. Philadelphia, PA: University of Pennsylvania Press.

11
WRITING UP

Kevin Ward

Introduction

This final chapter turns to the writing up of your research. As Northedge (1990: 156) notes, 'writing can ... be an extremely satisfying activity'. And so it can. There will be times when the words flow, when at the end of the working day you pat yourself on the back and say, 'well done' or 'good job'. However, the writing-up process can also be very annoying, demanding and frustrating! For Wolcott (1990: 12), 'Writing is always challenging and sometimes satisfying, but that is about as far as I can go in singing its praises.' I have been through the process of writing a dissertation four times. While on the one hand each has got progressively easier, as I have learnt from previous experiences and benefited from the advice of others, the production of each dissertation has still been hard! Trying to assemble all the pieces you have generated into something that you would be happy to call a dissertation is just plain difficult – although it is also extremely rewarding. Its writing – from the introduction to the literature review and the discussion of methods, to the representation of the 'data' and its analysis, and right through to the conclusion – is not something that is left to the end of the research process. The writing of the dissertation is instead something you have actually been doing since you began reading articles, taking notes and reflecting on the focus of your research. As Hennink et al. (2011: 273) put it:

> You will normally have the original project proposal document, some form of literature review, you may have kept notes, memos or a field diary during your data collection and may also have analytic notes, summaries ... Therefore, you already have a whole body of writing on your research project, and you rarely start with a truly 'blank page'.

Along the research journey – from the initial idea or thought to the submission of the dissertation – you have made certain decisions that have determined the material you now find yourself with. As Becker (1986: 16) notes, before we think we are turning to writing for the first time:

> Our earlier choices – to look at it this way, to think about this example in developing our ideas and storing data, to read this novel or watch that television program – rule out what we might otherwise have chosen. Every time we answer a question about our work and what we have been finding or thinking, our choice of words affects the way we describe it next time, perhaps when we are writing notes or making outlines.

This volume has outlined seven different ways of generating 'data'. These are the ones that are most widely used in the researching of the city. It has also revealed that there is some variability in what constitutes or counts as data. As this volume shows, in some cases it is constituted of words generated by someone else (see Chapters 3 and 7), or words you have generated in interacting with someone else (see Chapters 3 and 5), or numbers generated by someone else (see Chapter 9), or numbers you have generated interacting with someone else (see Chapter 6), or diaries/images/videos (see Chapters 8 and 10). Regardless of the nature of the data, according to Cloke et al. (2004), there are some common issues upon which you should reflect. That is, all data

> whatever their source, are *constructed* in one way another. They do not magically or spontaneously arise in the world just waiting for the geographer to come along; rather, they are 'made' by somebody for given reasons and in specific ways. (2004: 35, original emphasis)

So, regardless of the type of 'data' you are using – whether you are working with existing data, 'pre-constructed' in the words of Cloke et al. (2004), or data you have generated yourself, 'self-constructed'(ibid) – it is important you note and reflect upon how the data was produced and for what purpose. Data in whatever form is never neutral, and thus all of us need to think carefully about how and when we use it and the claims we make around it. Think about the issues covered in this book. The chapters have covered a variety of issues related to different aspects of the city and in each case the data has been generated in a particular context, from the funding behind its production through to the ways it has been disseminated.

It is not only that you need to reflect about the origins of your data and the dynamics behind its production. As I hope has also been clear as you have read through this book, the decision to choose a particular method to generate data is not one that should be made in splendid isolation. Each method comes with its own baggage, so to speak. That is, in choosing one or more methods to use in your dissertation you need to reflect on the questions you want to ask and answer, the categories you wish to use, and the types of knowledge (and data) you wish to generate. An example here might be appropriate. For my first MA dissertation I wanted to know about how undergraduate students travelled to university, across the city, and to calculate their value of time. On identifying and reading the existing literature in this field I generated a series of questions that I believed could be answered over the course of a few months – which was how long I had to conduct my research. Drawing on the work of others it seemed to me that a mixture of questionnaires and short semi-structured interviews would allow me to answer my questions. This would generate 'data' in the form of words and numbers. These were analysed, the latter in the form of a particular mathematical model, the former through printing the transcribed interviews and using highlighter pens (this was before ATLAS and other computer packages!). I then discussed my findings in relation to other similar studies. So, the choice of methods was one made in relation to other aspects of my study. Think about the methods you have used to generate material for your dissertation. Reflect on why you made the choice you did.

What is also worth taking from my example is that in making informed choices, whether about the case study, the constitution of data, the methods and so on, it is useful to be able to visualize the research process in its entirety – from reading the work of other academics through to analysing the data generated – from the beginning. Know what is involved in each aspect and divide up the time you have accordingly: that way you will have a sense of whether you are ahead, behind or on time in relation to your final submission deadline. That does not mean things do not change over the course of conducting research. They often do of course, as you have probably discovered! Rather, it has meant I hope anticipating and planning your research; that is, identifying the 'risks', so to speak, in your piece of research and to mitigate them as best you can in advance (see Chapter 2, this volume).

Regardless of which of the methods you use to research your city or cities in producing a dissertation, whether it be at the undergraduate or graduate level, you will reach the time you have allotted to 'writing up'. I have put this in quotes because it is not always clear what is meant by 'writing up' and when it should start. The purpose of this chapter is to provide some insights into how you might think about writing your dissertation and in the process to challenge the notion that 'writing up' is something you do towards the end of the research process. It is not, I would argue, 'the last … step of the research process' (Kumar 2011: 27). Instead, and reinforcing some of the comments I outlined in Chapter 2, this chapter makes the case for not understanding the research process as linear, as if the different elements should be added one to each other to produce a final product, the dissertation. That may well be how it looks from a typical dissertation contents page (see Figure 11.1).

Chapter One	Introduction	↓
Chapter Two	Academic literature review	↓
Chapter Three	Methodology	↓
Chapter Four	Empirical results/data and analysis I	↓
Chapter Five	Empirical results/data and analysis II	↓
Chapter Six	Conclusion	↓

Figure 11.1   A dissertation contents page

You have probably seen dissertations at your own institution in which the contents page seems to reflect this process, and Figure 11.1 is likely to resemble what you imagine your own contents page will look like. That is fine. This is a structure. However, this representation of the production of the dissertation – from introduction through to conclusion – is not actually how it was assembled. Rather, this chapter argues that the process of producing a dissertation on the city is non-linear. It is instead a process in which different elements are generated in tandem. As you are experiencing, producing a dissertation is an exercise in multi-tasking and time management. At different stages, 'writing' will take up more or less of your time. It will range from taking notes to jotting down thoughts, to producing fully formed and referenced sentences. And, at various times, you will move between the different elements of the dissertation and its writing, so that, as is the case made here, instead of a straight line, the writing of a dissertation more closely resembles a series of loops, as depicted in Figure 11.2.

This reflects how most of you will have conducted your research so far. The advantages of thinking about the research process in this way, are threefold, aside from it actually reflecting how most dissertations are produced and thus being a research design based more squarely on your own experiences. First, within this model there is the capacity for feedback and learning. That is, at each stage of the research process there is scope to return to work already produced and to reflect on it, add, edit and so on. So, each of the elements of the dissertation is constantly in conversation with the others throughout its production. The generating of the dissertation is an iterative process. This only stops when the dissertation is submitted for assessment. A second advantage of this approach is the explicit recognition that existing work – whether produced by academics or others – has its place across the dissertation, not just in the 'literature review' chapter. Most dissertations involve drawing upon and engaging with a series of existing literatures. Too many students review the work of others in just that chapter alone, failing to engage with existing methodological literatures throughout the dissertation. Moreover, the theoretical literatures discussed in the second chapter of many undergraduate and graduate dissertations should also be included in other chapters. So, where the data – whatever forms it takes – are included and discussed it makes sense to reference back to previous chapters and also to cite existing theoretical literature as a means of situating your own contribution. This is all part of the process of 'writing up' the dissertation, which is discussed in more detail in the next section. The third advantage to this approach is that the writing process is one of 'adjusting and refining' (Murray and Hughes 2008: 100). Thus the writing up of the dissertation is a process of experimentation, in which there is scope to make mistakes, to learn from them and still to produce a dissertation, as we will now see.

AL/RQ Academic literature/research questions
RD   Research design
GGA   Gathering, generating and analysing data
WU   Writing up

AL/RQ RD GGA WU   AL/RQ RD GGA WU   AL/RQ RD GGA WU   AL/RQ RD GGA WU   AL/RQ RD GGA WU   AL/RQ RD GGA WU

Figure 11.2 Writing a dissertation

Writing strategies

Having drawn together and assembled the different pieces into something called a dissertation, the task you now face is to begin the last stages of writing and rewriting (and rewriting and rewriting and …). There are a number of social science textbooks that claim to have the solution to the challenges all of us face when it comes to getting words down on a page and manipulating those we have already generated until you are happy. I am always deeply suspicious of any publication that proclaims to be able solve the issues most of us will face in writing a substantial piece of work, whether it is an undergraduate or graduate dissertation or an academic research monograph. The bottom line is that there is no simple solution to the writing up of any piece of research. Rather there are strategies that should hopefully make your life a little easier.

In thinking about writing up as more than just the final act of producing a 'polished' dissertation, it is worth emphasizing why it is more appropriate to think about the dissertation process as a series of loops as opposed to a straight line. First, thinking in terms of loops allows feedback to be introduced into the research process. For example, this means that as you conduct your fieldwork you may decide that research questions require reformulation. Or, as you analyse your 'data' you may express some dissatisfaction with your reading of the existing academic literature in your field. You may need to revisit it, or to incorporate other work from cognate areas, enlarging and then refining your theoretical focus. Second, in the traditional contents-page model of organizing and writing up the dissertation the existing

WRITING UP

work of academics is weakly positioned. There tends to be an assumption that it largely (and almost exclusively) figures in the 'literature review' chapter, which in many dissertations (such as the one outlined in Figure 11.1) is chapter 2. Of course, this is but one literature on which many of you will draw in writing your dissertation. Indeed, a strong piece of work will involve all of your chapters drawing upon the work of others to a greater or lesser extent. Think about your methods chapter. It will be expected that this will cover an outlining and rationalizing of your choice of methods. This will include situating your choice of methods in relation to wider philosophical concerns. To do this and not cite and draw upon existing literatures would seriously weaken your dissertation. Indeed, I doubt if any of the chapters you may have written so far have not made use of the work of academics. The 'analysis' chapters are also no exception. Representing your data and writing about your findings demand that you situate them *vis-à-vis* what others have found in similar studies. So, in writing your dissertation as a series of loops you are able to make better use of a wider set of literatures, and avoid the impression that drawing on existing work is something you do in one chapter only.

Third, in organizing the writing up of your dissertation according to a set of loops, you write the dissertation through a series of iterations. '[W]riting need not be a one-shot, all-or-nothing venture' according to Becker (1986: 14); rather, there is a need to allow room for clarification and editing, the moving of text and the general assembling, disassembling and reassembling of words, images, tables, figures and so on. Adopting this approach should reduce the pressure some of us put on ourselves to produce the perfect text first time around. That rarely happens. Going through iteration after iteration – with time built in to think about how the current version is different from, and hopefully better than, previous versions – is a more mature way of pulling together the various things you have produced and written during the course of the research process – which can be anything between nine and fifteen months, depending on your institution's programme.

Fourth, the tempo or rhythm of *when* and *what* you write requires some reflection. Here I am not talking quite literally about the speed at which you work, although that is important. No. Rather, and given what has already been written about the production of data and words in the dissertation, I hope it should not come as a surprise that you should think seriously about when best you write and what kinds of writing you do best and when. Some of those who have contributed chapters in this volume write better in the mornings. For others, they find it easier to articulate their thoughts late in the evening. Moreover, the differentiation can be more fine-grained than this suggests. I find it easier to edit and move text around in the evening, but to generate 'new' words in the morning. There is a need to take seriously the organizing of the writing process. This requires some honest reflection. For Cloke et al. (2004: 341), 'approaching writing as an ongoing part of the practice of human geography also means recognizing it needs to be organized.'

Fifth, it is worth reflecting on whether you might draw others into the production of your dissertation. Why? Well, because as Northedge (1990: 195) notes:

Although many of us feel impelled to treat writing as a very private activity, it is paradoxically also intrinsically a public activity. It is private in that we do it by ourselves, locked in our own thoughts and according to our own habits and perceptions, with very little idea of how other people cope with the challenges it presents. But it is also public in that what we are producing is intended to be read by others, perhaps strangers.

A word of caution here, however! A growing number of universities have plagiarism rules. This means that you have to sign to confirm that the dissertation you submit is your work and your work only. So, I am not suggesting that you co-write your dissertation, or worse, that you draw on the words of others without citing it in the appropriate manner. Rather, I mean that many of us write by ourselves – on our own, struggling with how to write and rewrite paragraph after paragraph, page after page. It does not have to be this way though. In your own institution you might have a member of staff who will read a draft of at least one chapter. That is clearly useful. However, you could think of going further, perhaps establishing a 'writing circle', in which students read one another's chapters, offering constructive advice and criticism. Or sometimes just having someone else, who does not need to be a student, read a copy of your work can be useful, in terms of identifying grammatical errors, stylistic issues and unclear sections. We all get very close to our work; we cannot see good and bad material for looking! This is especially the case as the clock ticks down and the pressure begins to mount. In this situation – which is one we are all probably familiar with – having a friendly reader may prove to be immensely useful.

Sixth, and finally, Wolcott (1990) provides some interesting insight into how best to approach the different aspects of writing up. Running through his four-fold schema is the following 'take home message': 'Hear this: *You cannot begin writing early enough*' (Wolcott 1990: 20, original emphasis). Perhaps not surprisingly he kicks things off with a section entitled 'getting going'. Reiterating the argument made earlier in this chapter, Wolcott notes that 'at the moment you generate sentences that could conceivably appear in your completed account, you have begun writing' (1990: 13), although I hope you notice that in this volume we are less concerned with the relationship between the words you have written down and the 'completed account'. He then moves on to 'keeping going'. At this stage he suggests obtaining some feedback on your work. As we have already discussed, getting someone else to read your work – so long as you are able to use the comments in a positive manner – is generally a good thing. The emphasis is on keeping the writing moving forward. Wolcott's third element is 'tightening up'. What does that mean, I hear some of you say? Well, it reinforces the argument made in this volume that the production of a dissertation is not a linear, additive process. Rather, moving back and forth between chapters – editing and re-editing, on the lookout for clarifying the meaning of sentences, the subtle shifting in emphasis, or the structural reorganizing of chapters – is incredibly time-consuming. Sometimes you know when you are done, although more often than not it is an external deadline that forces you to stop and to hand over your dissertation. The final aspect to Wolcott's (1990) schema is 'finishing up'. This literally means drawing a line under your dissertation and submitting it, although for many of you to do this also involves not just letting go of something you have become close to, and worked on for perhaps 9–12 months. It also means ensuring that you are familiar with how you should structure your dissertation. This need not be complicated but getting it right can be time-consuming. Indeed, it is hard to overestimate quite how long the 'tightening up' and 'finishing up' elements can – and often do – take.

Conclusion

In his book *Writing for Social Scientists* the sociologist Howard Becker (1986: 164) begins his final chapter with the following:

> Reading this book will not solve all of your writing problems. It will hardly solve any of them. No book, no author, no expert – no one else can solve your problems. They are yours. You have to get rid of them.

Strong words you may think. He subsequently proceeds to note, 'but you might get some ideas about how to solve them'. I would say the same about *Researching the City*. This book will not solve the problems you are likely to face when you decide to research the city, for cities are complicated combinations and outcomes of a range of cultural, economic, environmental, social, political and technological processes. That they are complicated in this way – and others too – is also what makes them the subject of so many dissertations each year at universities around the world.

The challenges that all of us face, including academics with well-established careers, in researching the city are there regardless of the choice of method or methods. You were probably aware of some these before you began reading. Maybe that was why you chose to read this volume! However, it may have highlighted some challenges or issues that you may not have realized you were going to face or have to overcome! That would be unfortunate but not a surprise. No one can foresee at the beginning of the research process all the issues they will encounter during the course of conducting an urban research project. However, the hope is that the various contributions included here have provided you with a series of insights into how you might best anticipate and manage them. Whether it is Stephen Ward (Chapter 3) discussing his time spent in and amongst urban planning archives, Nik Theodore (Chapter 6) outlining how he and his team managed to access and study some of the most marginal inhabitants of US cities, or Bradley Garrett (Chapter 10) revealing what he got up to while spending time with urban explorers, whose subterranean antics occur where and when most of us are not looking, the various chapters have provided a mix of insights into the methodological and theoretical assumptions that accompany the use of particular methods as well as some more grounded instructions into their actual use.

Whether ethnography, discourse analysis, GIS or interviewing, each chapter has outlined why you might want to use a particular method. They have discussed the sorts of data the methods generate and the kinds of questions they are best suited to answer. For what should be clear is that the method or methods you choose to use to study the city (or cities) is, or are, embedded in a wider set of decisions you make. These range from the aspects of cities that most interest you and when you plan to conduct your research, through to more prosaic concerns over the kinds of questions you wish to answer and the theoretical perspectives that you find most persuasive.

In conclusion, the hope above all else is that in deciding to research the city you realize what a good choice you have made. For while this volume has introduced a series of methods, which each in its own way renders the city simpler and thus more easily researchable, it is important that we do not lose sight of the incredible richness of cities. Although there is likely to be a lot at stake in your dissertation – at Geography at the University of Manchester they count for one-eighth of the overall mark for undergraduates – I hope that in researching your particular city or cities you also learn something about yourself. For the choices you have made along the way also speak to your character and personality. As we saw earlier in the volume (see Chapter 2), the producing of an undergraduate or graduate dissertation is about your abilities in the wider sense, including, but not exclusively, your academic ability. So, good luck with your studies and remember that the images, numbers or words that you use in your dissertation represent events, lives, places and so on that matter to people. As you produce a dissertation for your degree, reflect on the responsibility you have to those whose experiences or views form the basis of your study.

References

Becker, H.S. (1986) *Writing for Social Scientists.* Chicago, IL: University of Chicago Press.

Cloke, P., Cook, I., Crang, P., Goodwin, M., Painter, J. and Philo, C. (2004) *Practising Human Geography.* London: Sage.

Hennink, M., Hutter, I. and Bailey, A. (2011) *Qualitative Research Methods.* London: Sage.

Kumar, R. (2011) *Research Methodology: A Step-by-Step Guide for Beginners.* London: Sage.

Murray, N. and Hughes, G. (2008) *Writing Up Your University Assignments and Research Projects: A Practical Handbook.* Maidenhead: Open University Press.

Northedge, A. (1990) *The Good Study Guide.* Milton Keynes: Open University Press.

Walliman, N. (2011) *Your Research Project: Designing and Planning Your Work* (3rd edn). London: Sage.

Wolcott, H.F. (1990) *Writing Up Qualitative Research.* London: Sage.

INDEX

Pages denoting figures and tables are marked in italics.